Editorial Project Manager
Lorin E. Klistoff, M.A.

Editor in Chief
Ina Massler Levin, M.A.

Illustrator
Kelly McMahon

Cover Artist
Brenda DiAntonis

Creative Director
Karen J. Goldfluss, M.S. Ed.

Art Production Manager
Kevin Barnes

Art Coordinator
Renée Christine Yates

Imaging
James Edward Grace
Craig Gunnell

Publisher
Mary D. Smith, M.S. Ed.

W9-BUQ-779

Authors

Franka Chavez-Rodriguez,
Mayra Saenz-Ulloa, M.A.,
and Sabrina Mastromarco-Diaz

Teacher Created Resources, Inc.
6421 Industry Way
Westminster, CA 92683
www.teachercreated.com
ISBN: 978-1-4206-2076-4
© 2008 Teacher Created Resources, Inc.
Made in U.S.A.

Teacher Created Resources

Table of Contents

Table of Contents

Introduction

Reading is essentially the fundamental tool to all academic success. *Word Family Activities: Short Vowels* addresses the standards for reading skills, while assisting test preparation in enriching and creative ways. In recent years, there has been an increasingly strong emphasis on teaching word families in the primary curriculum in order to meet the demands of developing fluent readers. This book addresses the K–1 grade level, and the activities are extremely teacher/student friendly. It is designed with large print for young learners, along with simple identifiable pictures to help assist English language learners. The activities in part 1 are designed to build student success in word family knowledge using a very basic understanding. This allows proper scaffolding to take place during a teacher's instruction. Part 2 activities lead into challenging the learner's knowledge during student independent work time. This section allows the learner to manipulate the sounds in each of the word families. Part 3 ensures that students are able to read, write, and identify word families. Additional resources are also included to further assist instruction.

 Standards

Word Family Activities: Short Vowels meets the following language arts standard and benchmarks for the K–1 grades classroom. (Used with permission from McREL. Copyright 2004 McREL. Mid-continent Research for Education and Learning. 2550 S. Parker Road, Suite 500, Aurora, CO 80014. Telephone (303) 337-0990. Website: www.mcrel.org/standards-benchmarks.)

Standard 5: Uses the general skills and strategies of the reading process

- Uses basic elements of phonetic analysis (e.g., common letter/sound relationships, beginning and ending consonants, vowel sounds, blends, word patterns) to decode unknown words

- Uses basic elements of structural analysis (e.g., syllables, basic prefixes, suffixes, root words, compound words, spelling patterns, contractions) to decode unknown words

---

Short A

-an
-ap
-at

5

Part 1: Short A
Teacher Support/Home Support

Activity Directions

Flashcards (pages 7 and 8 or 9 and 10 or 11 and 12)

Copy the set of flashcards that you want the students to learn back to back (pages 7 and 8 or pages 9 and 10 or pages 11 and 12). Make sure the cards align properly when copying.

Have students trace and rewrite "short a" words on side A along with reading the words aloud. Side B will allow students to draw their own interpretations of the words. Students will then cut out the cards and place them on a ring for review or use them as a reference.

Letter Slide (pages 13, 14, or 15)

Teacher precuts dashed lines inside picture. Students will cut the strips of letters. Students insert the letter strips to create and manipulate "short a" words.

(*Note:* Students can independently ask other classmates to read the words created with the letter slide.)

Blending Boxes (pages 16, 17, or 18)

First, inform students that they will be building words by listening for beginning, middle, and ending sounds. For example, in *cat,* the *c* can be changed to *h* to create *hat.* Next, the teacher stretches out the word. Both student and teacher repeat the word slowly. Then, the teacher will ask questions to help guide students to develop the sounds to write in the proper boxes. Lastly, students blend the sounds while connecting the dots to show directionality. Students read the words and practice writing them on the line.

Beginning Sound Substitution (pages 19, 20, or 21)

Students cross out the beginning sound to create a new "short a" word. Use the pictures on the left as a guide. Have students read the words as they create them. The teacher must inform students that they are only substituting the beginning sound to create a new word.

pan

ran

can

man

fan

van

pan

ran

can

man

fan

van

lap

cap

nap

map

zap

tap

9

cap

lap

map

nap

tap

zap

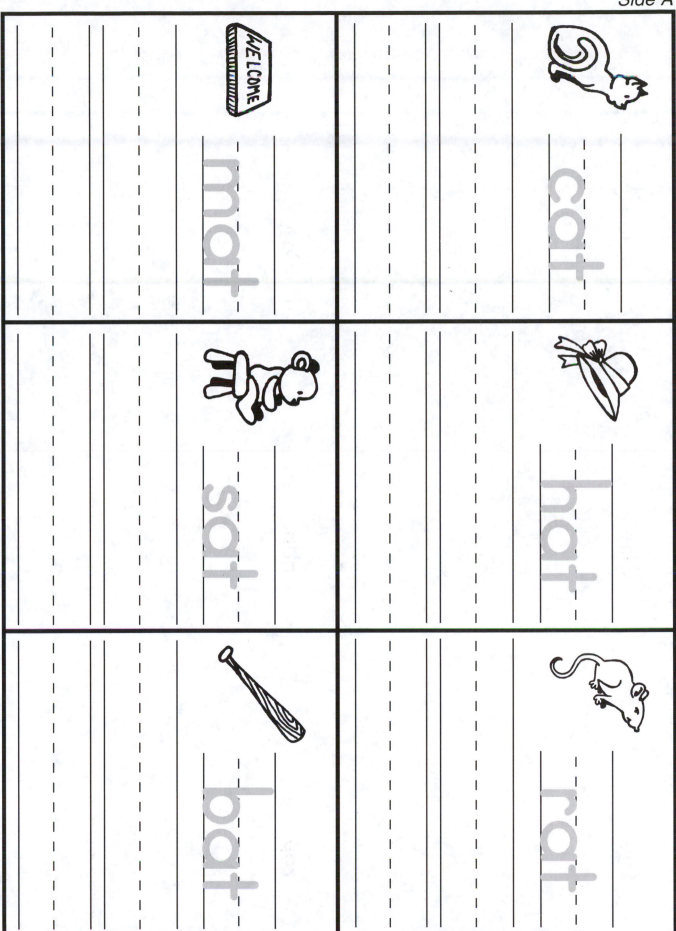

cat

mat

hat

sat

rat

bat

cat

mat

hat

sat

rat

bat

Letter Slide

Cut the strip of letters. Cut the slits on the van. Insert the strip of letters to create and manipulate the –an words.

p c f r m v

an

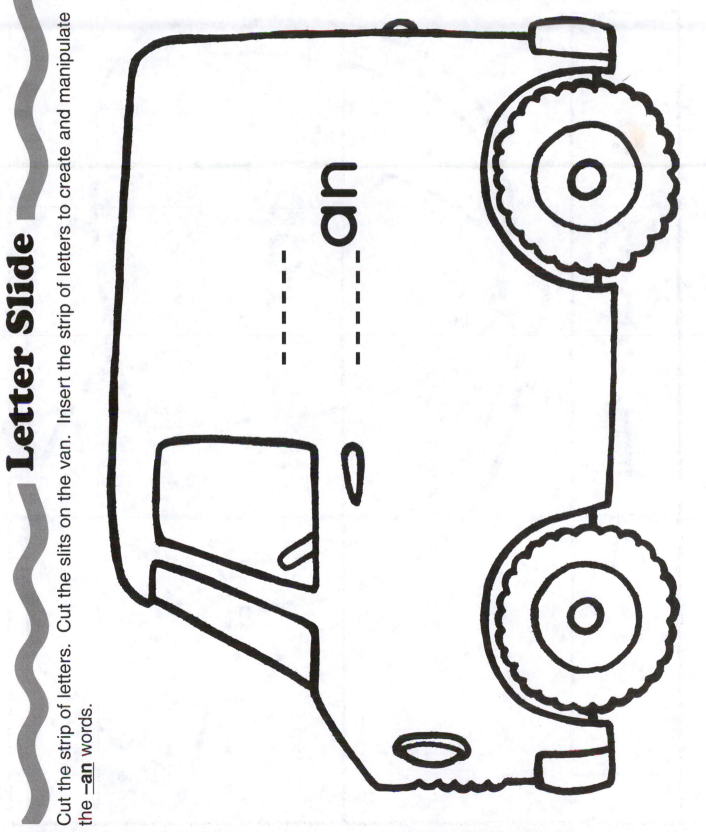

Letter Slide

Cut the strip of letters. Cut the slits on the cap. Insert the strip of letters to create and manipulate the **–ap** words.

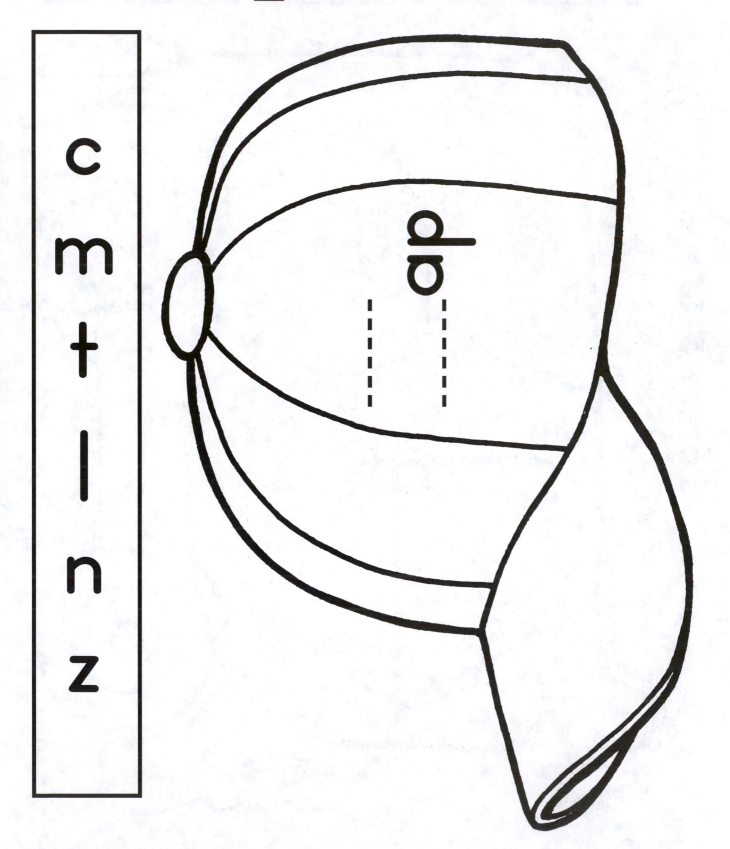

Letter Slide

Cut the strip of letters. Cut the slits on the cat. Insert the strip of letters to create and manipulate the **–at** words.

_ _ _ _ _ _
_ _ _ _ _ at

c
b
h
r
m
s

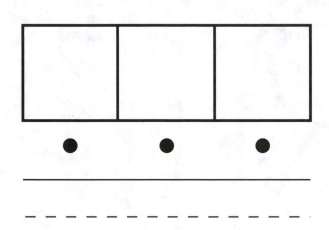

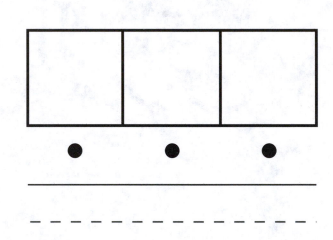

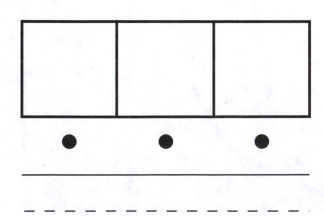

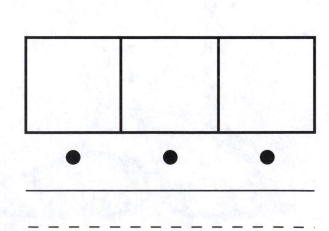

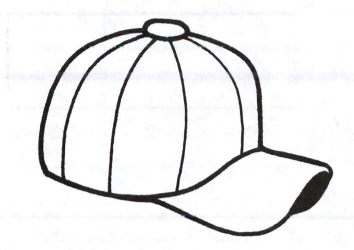

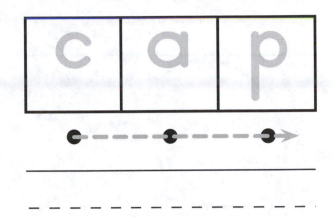

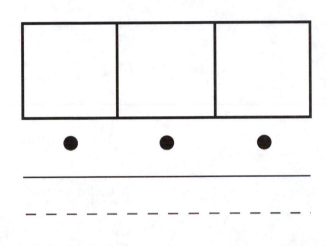

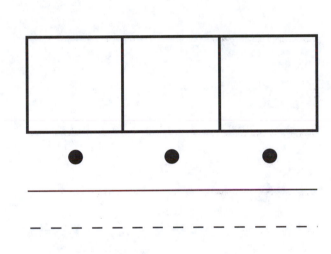

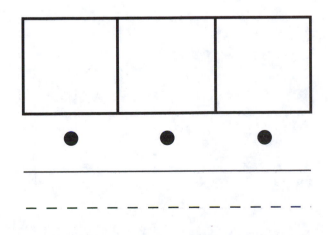

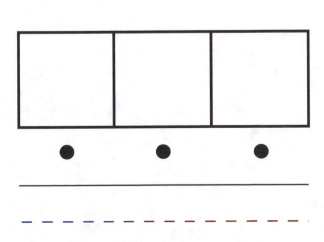

 # Blending Boxes

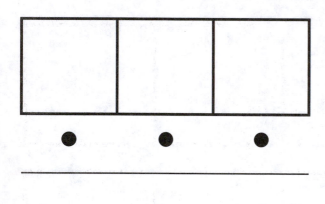

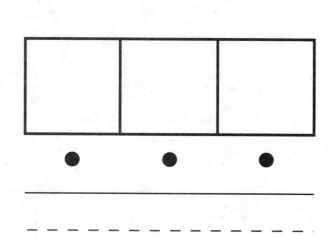

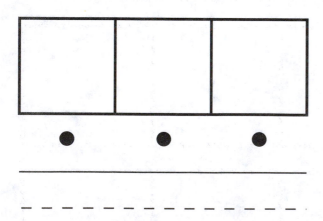

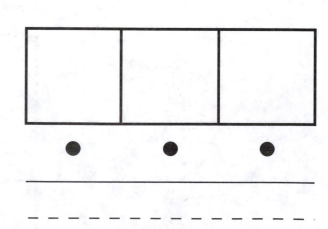

Beginning Sound Substitution

Cross out the beginning sound to create a new **–an** word. Use the pictures on the left as a guide.

Beginning Sound Substitution

Cross out the beginning sound to create a new **–ap** word. Use the pictures on the left as a guide.

Beginning Sound Substitution

Cross out the beginning sound to create a new **–at** word. Use the pictures on the left as a guide.

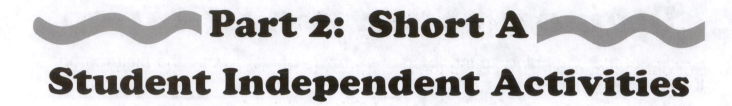

Part 2: Short A
Student Independent Activities

Activity Directions

Building Words (pages 23, 24, or 25)

Cut out the letter boxes. Glue the letters in the correct boxes to create words that match the corresponding pictures.

Flip Book (pages 26–28 for –*an*, 29–31 for –*ap*, or 32–34 for –*at*)

Copy page 2 and the "My Picture" page back to back. Make sure the dashed lines are aligned. Then copy page 1.

First, fold page 2 along the solid line and only cut the dashed lines.

Second, cut and glue the pictures from page 1 onto the flip book (page 2).

Third, have students draw their own pictures where it says "My Picture" in the inside.

Fourth, cut out the letter boxes from page 1. Glue letters to the corresponding pictures to make the correct CVC words.

Fifth, have students write the CVC words two more times.

Mystery Picture (pages 35, 36, or 37)

Find and color the "short a" words to discover the mystery picture. Once the mystery picture is discovered, students will then write the "short a" mystery word in the sentence below the picture.

Word Search (pages 38, 39, or 40)

Find and color the "short a" words. Have students write the "short a" words that are found in the word search in the empty spaces below.

Building Words

Cut out the letters below. Glue them in the correct boxes to create words that match the **–an** pictures.

Building Words

Cut out the letters below. Glue them in the correct boxes to create words that match the **–ap** pictures.

Building Words

Cut out the letters below. Glue them in the correct boxes to create words that match the **–at** pictures.

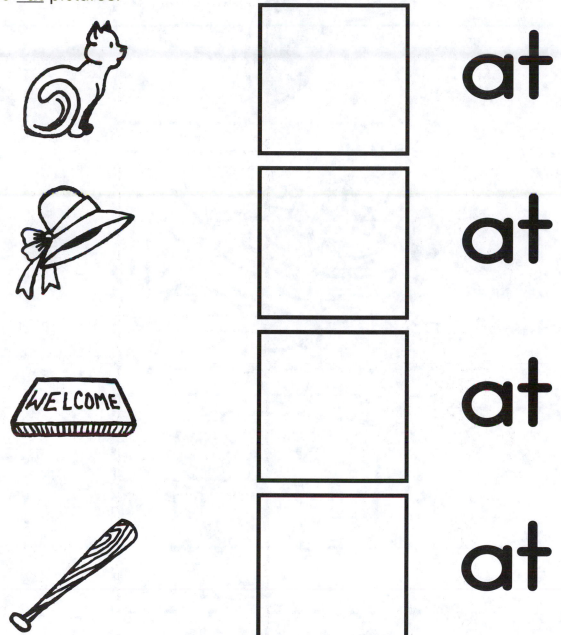

Flip Book (–an)

Cut out the pictures and letters below.

Glue them on the flip book.

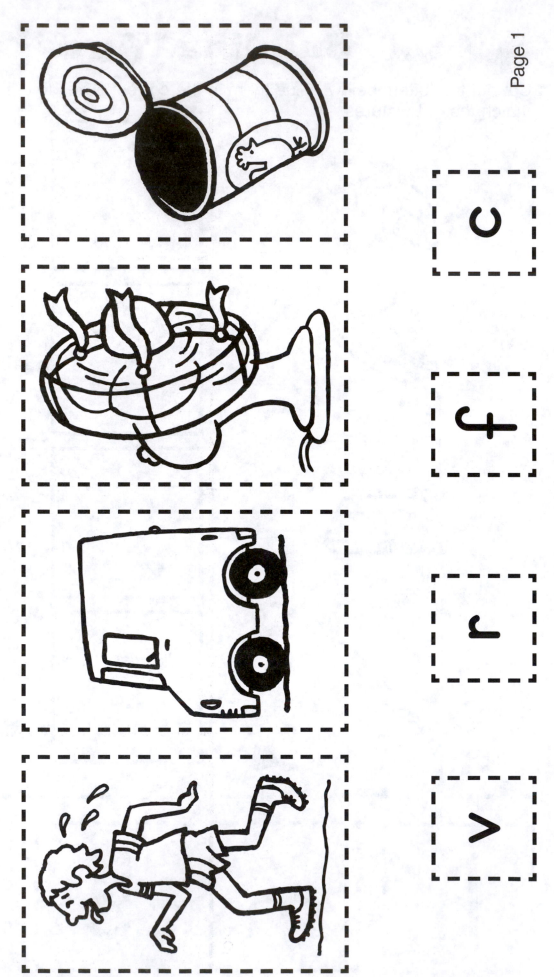

26

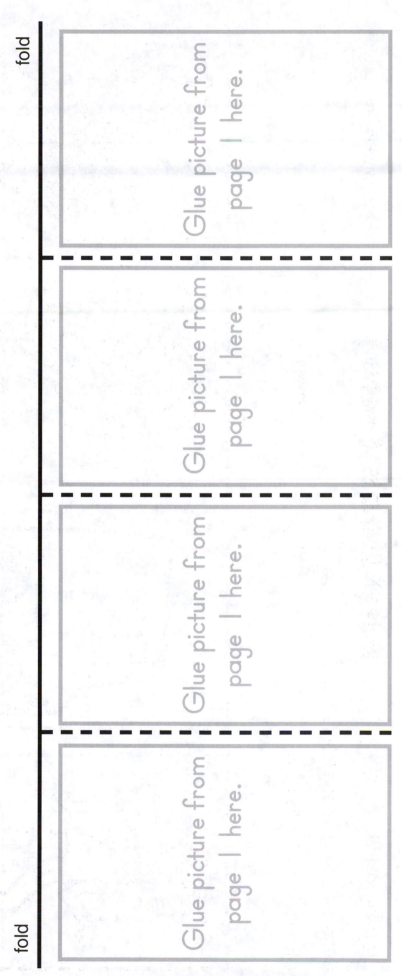

fold

Glue picture from page 1 here.

Glue picture from page 1 here.

Glue picture from page 1 here.

Glue picture from page 1 here.

fold

My Picture

My Picture

My Picture

My Picture

an

an

an

an

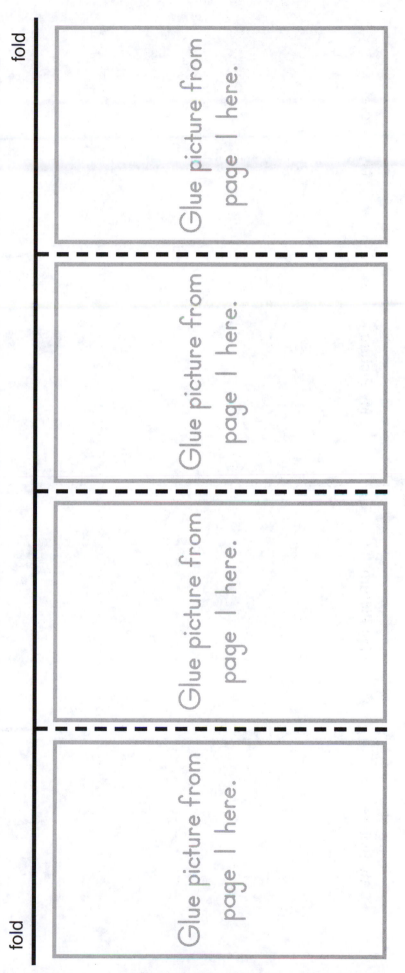

My Picture

My Picture

My Picture

My Picture

ap

ap

ap

ap

Flip Book (–ap)

Cut out the pictures and letters below.

Glue them on the flip book.

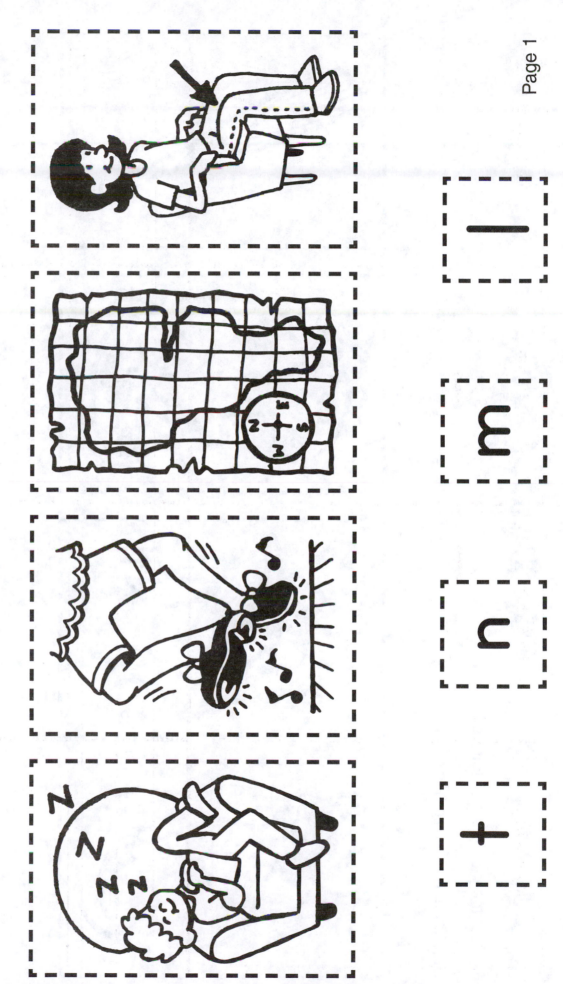

| l |
| m |
| n |
| t |

Flip Book (–at)

Cut out the pictures and letters below.

Glue them on the flip book.

32   ©Teacher Created Resources, Inc.

fold

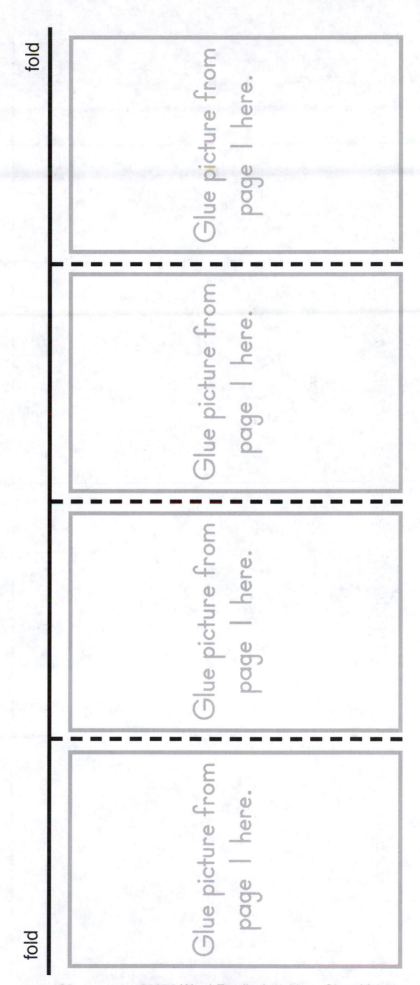

Glue picture from page 1 here.

Glue picture from page 1 here.

Glue picture from page 1 here.

Glue picture from page 1 here.

fold

My Picture

My Picture

My Picture

My Picture

at

at

at

at

Mystery Picture

Color the spaces with the **–an** pictures green to discover the mystery picture. Color the other spaces blue.

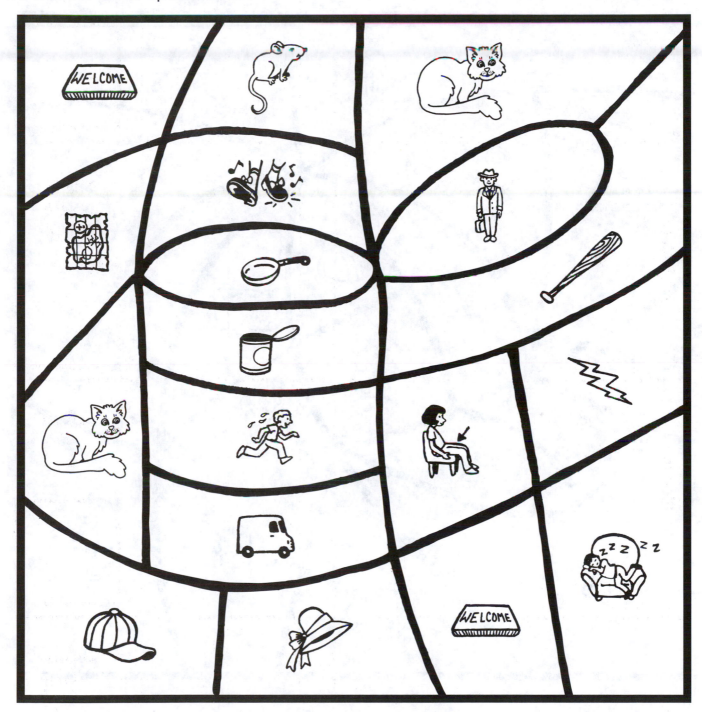

I see a _____ .

Mystery Picture

Color the spaces with the **–ap** pictures red to discover the mystery picture.
Color the other spaces black.

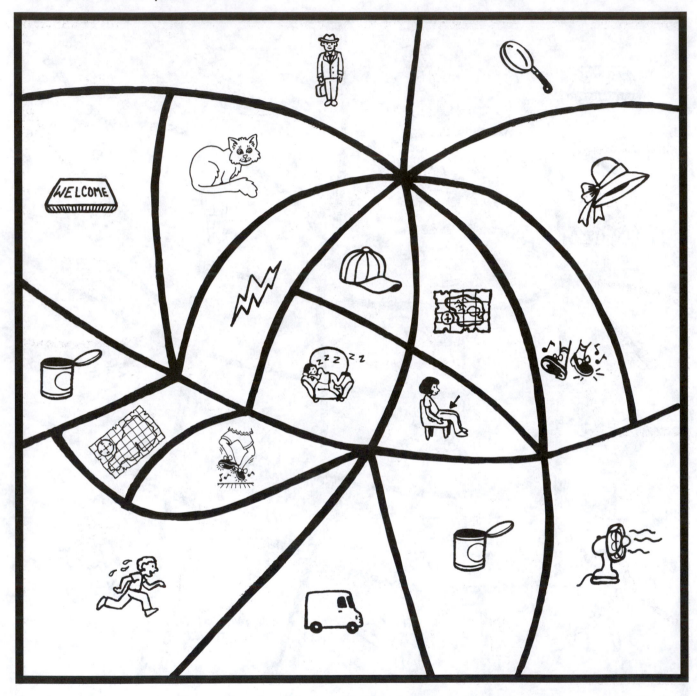

I like my _____ .

Mystery Picture

Color the spaces with the **–at** pictures brown to discover the mystery picture.
Color the other spaces green.

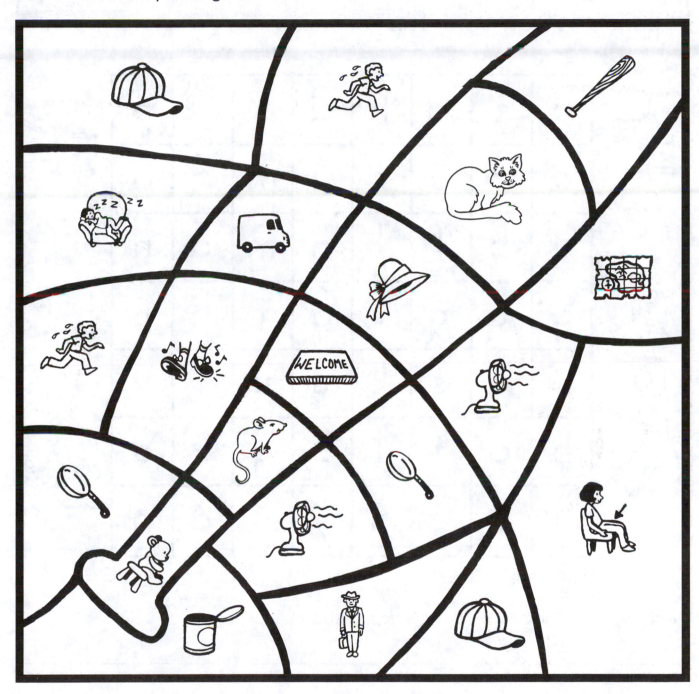

I see a _____ .

Word Search

Find and color the **–an** words.

pan	can	fan	ran	man	van

c	f	a	n	d	s	t	p
c	m	c	r	u	m	f	a
u	b	f	l	h	m	a	n
a	u	q	v	a	t	h	u
n	g	s	k	u	u	t	v
b	a	t	l	b	g	z	a
h	c	a	n	y	r	a	n

Write the **–an** words that you have found above.

_____   _____   _____

_____   _____   _____

_____   _____   _____

Word Search

Find and color the **–ap** words.

cap	map	lap	nap	zap	tap

c	f	a	m	a	p	s	p
c	m	c	r	u	m	f	x
l	b	f	l	h	m	a	n
a	u	q	n	a	t	h	u
p	z	s	k	u	a	t	v
b	a	t	n	a	p	z	r
h	p	a	p	y	c	a	p

Write the **–ap** words that you have found above.

_____ _____ _____

_____ _____ _____

Word Search

Find and color the **–at** words.

cat	mat	bat	rat	sat	hat

c	a	t	x	d	e	p	g
c	m	c	r	u	m	f	e
s	b	f	l	h	a	t	j
a	u	q	v	i	t	h	u
t	g	s	k	u	u	t	g
b	a	t	l	b	g	z	i
h	h	u	g	y	r	a	t

Write the **–at** words that you have found in the word search.

_____   _____   _____

_____   _____   _____

Part 3: Short A
Word Family Review

Activity Directions

Word Sort (pages 42 and 43)

Students will sort CVC words in the correct columns.

(*Extension:* Have students read the CVC words to classmates.)

Make, Read, and Write CVC Words (page 44)

Students cut out the letter and picture cards on the dashed lines. Students manipulate letter cards to form CVC words. Students then read the words and find the matching pictures. Lastly, students may use blank paper to write the CVC words they have formed. Use plastic baggies or envelopes to store letters and pictures.

Fluency Practice (page 45)

Students read the randomly placed "short a" CVC words from top to bottom. Sand timers may be given to students to time how many words they can read in the given time.

My Own CVC Words (page 46)

Students will write their own "short a" CVC words on the lines provided. They can read and share their words with classmates.

(*Note:* Students can also cut on the solid lines to make flashcards.)

Making Sentences with CVC Words (pages 47, 48, or 49)

Students will cut out the "short a" CVC words and glue them in the boxes to make sentences. They can use the picture clues. Students should be encouraged to read their sentences aloud.

Word Sort

1. Cut out the **short a** words.

2. Glue each word in the correct column on the following page.

3. Be careful. There are some words that do not belong to the word families.
   Can you find them?

can	cap	bat	jam	hat
tap	van	rat	hug	mom
sat	ran	star	hut	lap
sad	dad	bat	pan	nap
man	mat	tap	zap	van

-at	-an	-ap

Make, Read, and Write CVC Words

Cut along the lines. Make, read, and write **short a** words.

a	t	r	h	c
m	b	s	n	v
r	f	z	l	p

44

Fluency Practice

Read	Read	Read	Read
hat	zap	pan	tap	tan	nap
cat	lap	nap	tap	sat	pan
rat	map	rat	van	lap	cat
mat	tap	ran	fat	man	cap
sat	hat	zap	map	mat	can
bat	can	mat	fan	zap	hat
fat	cap	man	bat	ran	tap
can	cat	lap	map	rat	map

Read	Read
pan	—
ran	—
man	—
tan	—
fan	—
van	—
cap	—
nap	—

My Own CVC Words (short a)

CVC CVC CVC	CVC CVC
CVC CVC CVC	CVC CVC
CVC CVC CVC	CVC CVC
CVC CVC CVC	CVC CVC

Making Sentences with CVC Words

Cut out the _-an_ words below. Glue them in the correct boxes to create sentences. Read the sentences aloud.

1. I see a ☐.

2. I like my ☐.

3. I have a ☐.

4. I can see a ☐.

---

van   fan   can   pan

Cut out the **-ap** words below. Glue them in the correct boxes to create sentences. Read the sentences aloud.

1. I see a [ ].

2. I like to [ ].

3. I have a [ ].

4. I can [ ].

map   cap   tap   nap

Making Sentences with CVC Words

Cut out the **-at** words below. Glue them in the correct boxes to create sentences. Read the sentences aloud.

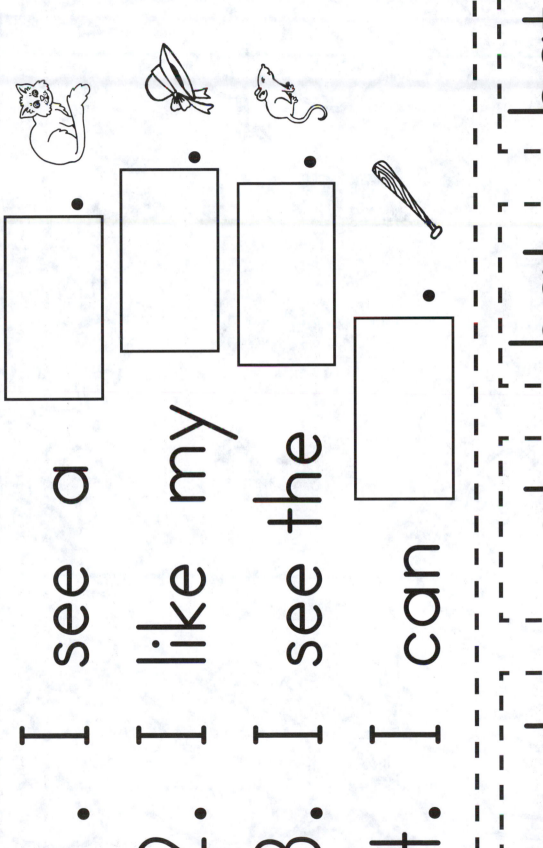

1. I see a ⬚

2. I like my ⬚

3. I see the ⬚

4. I can ⬚

rat cat

hat bat

Short E
-ed
-en
-et

Part 1: Short E
Teacher Support/Home Support

Activity Directions

Letter Slide (pages 52, 53, or 54)

Teacher precuts dashed lines inside picture. Students will cut the strips of letters. Students insert the letter strips to create and manipulate "short e" words.

(*Note:* Students can independently ask other classmates to read the words created with the letter slide.)

Flashcards (pages 55 and 56, pages 57 and 58, or pages 59 and 60)

Copy the set of flashcards that you want the students to learn back to back (pages 55 and 56, pages 57 and 58, or pages 59 and 60). Make sure the cards align properly when copying.

Have students trace and rewrite "short e" words on side A along with reading the words aloud. Side B will allow students to draw their own interpretations of the words. Students will then cut out the cards and place them on a ring for review or use them as a reference.

Blending Boxes (pages 61, 62, or 63)

First, inform students that they will be building words by listening for beginning, middle, and ending sounds. For example, in *bed,* the *b* can be changed to *f* to create *fed.* Next, the teacher stretches out the word. Both student and teacher repeat the word slowly. Then, the teacher will ask questions to help guide students to develop the sounds to write in the proper boxes. Lastly, students blend the sounds while connecting the dots to show directionality. Students read the words and practice writing them on the line.

Beginning Sound Substitution (pages 64, 65, or 66)

Students cross out the beginning sound to create a new "short e" word. Use the pictures on the left as a guide. Have students read the words as they create them. The teacher must inform students that they are only substituting the beginning sound to create a new word.

Letter Slide

Cut the strip of letters. Cut the slits on the bed. Insert the strip of letters to create and manipulate the **-ed** words.

r
b
sh
f
T
sl

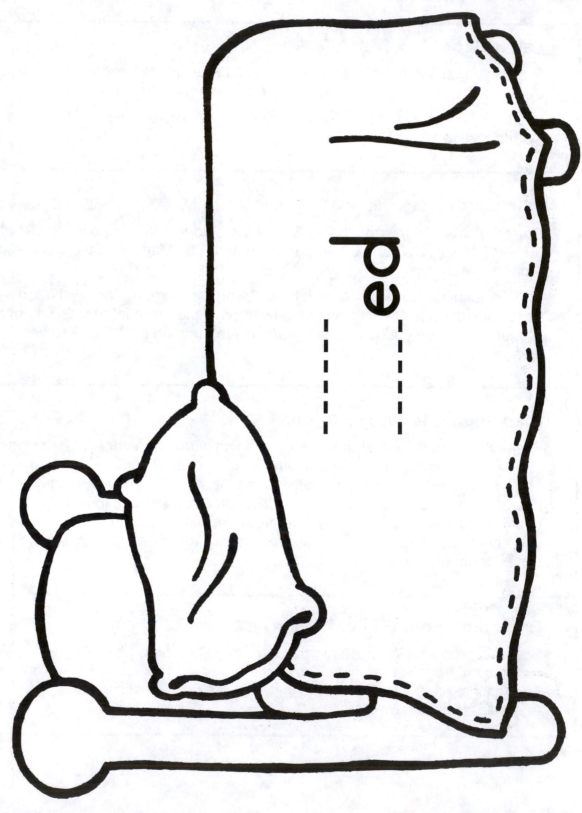

_ _ _ _ ed

Letter Slide

Cut the strip of letters. Cut the slits on the hen. Insert the strip of letters to create and manipulate the **–en** words.

_ _ _ _ _ _

_ _ _ _ _ en

h
p
t
B
d
m

Letter Slide

Cut the strip of letters. Cut the slits on the jet. Insert the strip of letters to create and manipulate the **–et** words.

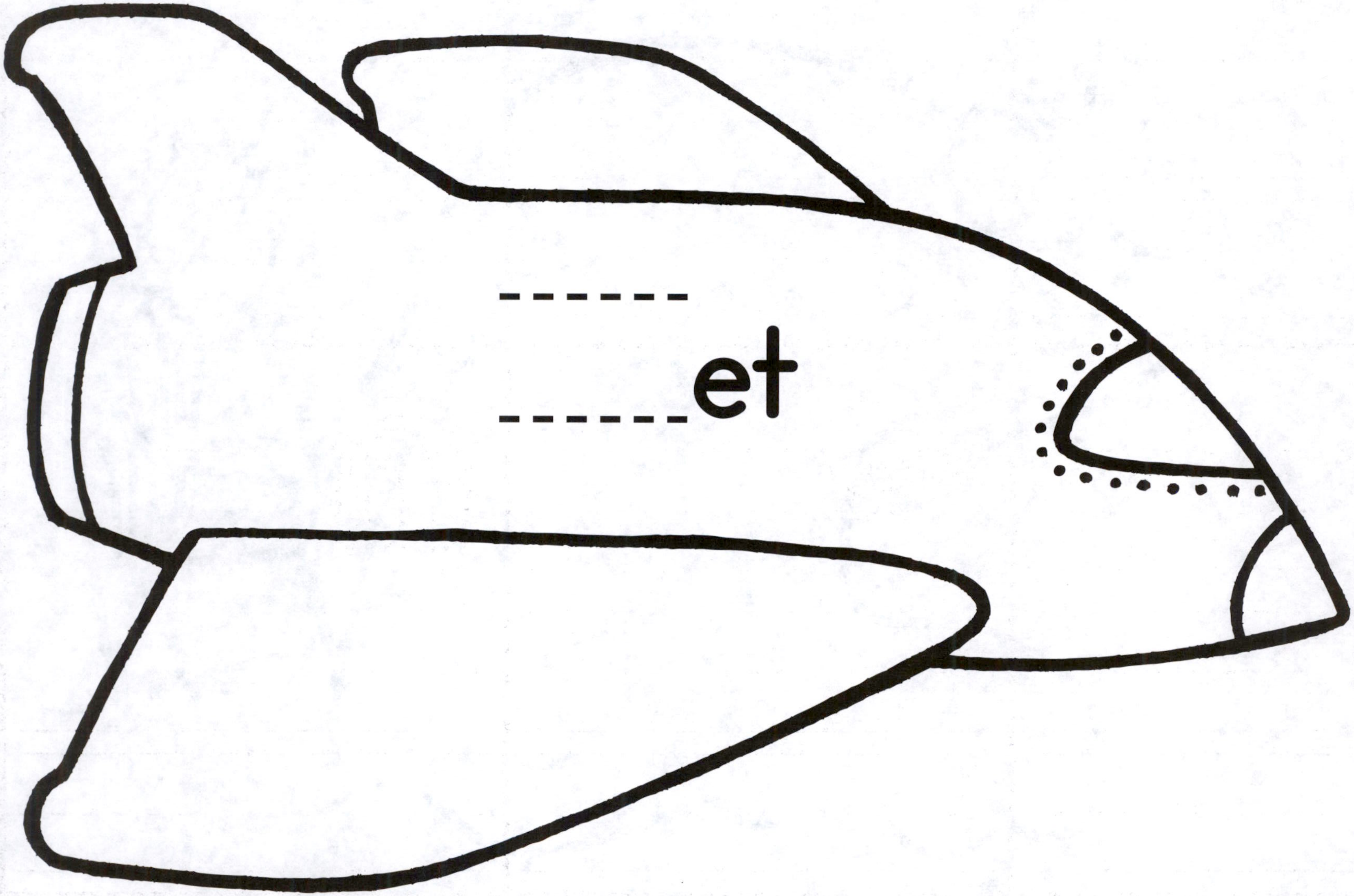

w
j
p
n
b
m

Ted

bed

sled

red

shed

fed

bed

Ted

red

sled

fed

shed

Ben

hen

den

pen

men

ten

hen

Ben

pen

den

ten

men

net

jet

bet

wet

met

pet

jet

net

wet

bet

pet

met

Blending Boxes

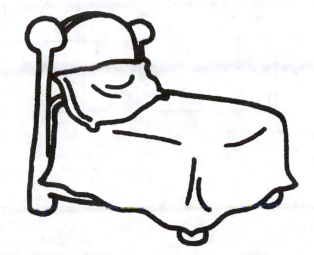

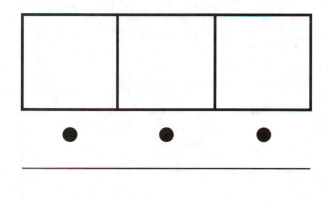

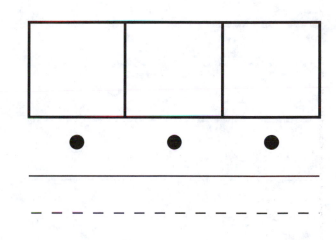

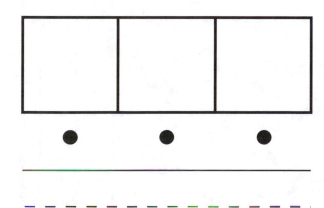

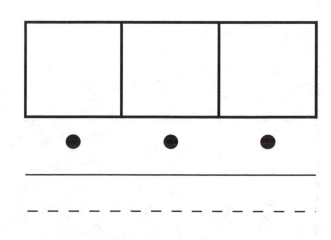

 # Blending Boxes

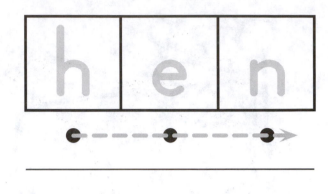

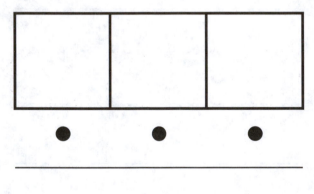

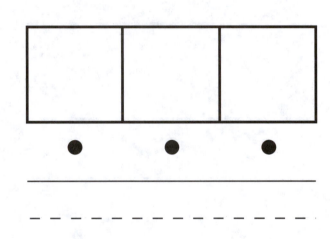

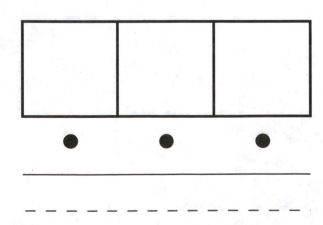

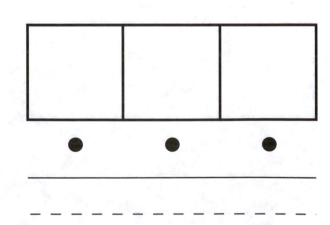

Blending Boxes

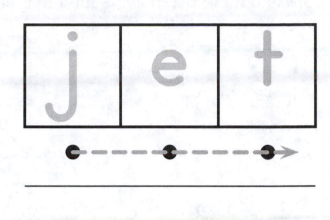

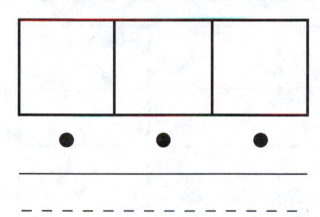

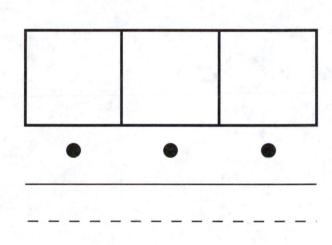

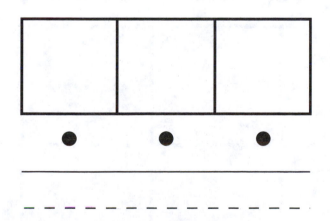

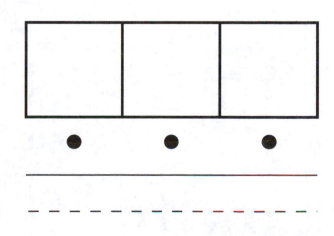

Beginning Sound Substitution

Cross out the beginning sound to create a new **–ed** word. Use the pictures on the left as a guide.

Beginning Sound Substitution

Cross out the beginning sound to create a new **–en** word. Use the pictures on the left as a guide.

Beginning Sound Substitution

Cross out the beginning sound to create a new __et__ word. Use the pictures on the left as a guide.

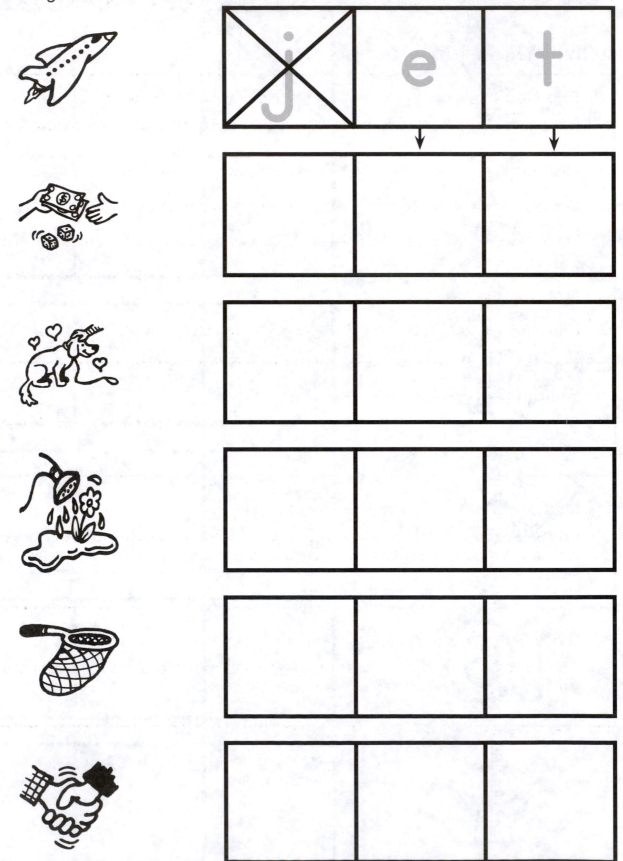

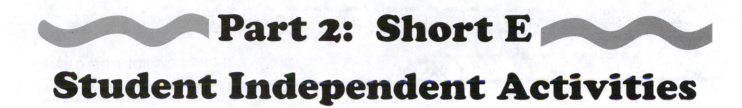

Part 2: Short E
Student Independent Activities

Activity Directions

Flip Book (pages 68–70 for *–ed*, 71–73 for *–en*, or 74–76 for *–et*)

Copy page 2 and the "My Picture" page back to back. Make sure the dashed lines are aligned. Then copy page 1.

First, fold page 2 along the solid line and only cut the dashed lines.

Second, cut and glue the pictures from page 1 onto the flip book (page 2).

Third, have students draw their own pictures where it says "My Picture" in the inside.

Fourth, cut out the letter boxes from page 1. Glue letters to the corresponding pictures to make the correct CVC words.

Fifth, have students write the CVC words two more times.

Building Words (pages 77, 78, or 79)

Cut out the letter boxes. Glue the letters in the correct boxes to create words that match the corresponding pictures.

Mystery Picture (pages 80, 81, or 82)

Find and color the "short e" words to discover the mystery picture. Once the mystery picture is discovered, students will then write the "short e" mystery word in the sentence below.

Word Search (pages 83, 84, or 85)

Find and color the "short e" words. Have students write the "short e" words that are found in the word search in the empty spaces below.

Flip Book (–ed)

Cut out the pictures and letters below.

Glue them on the flip book.

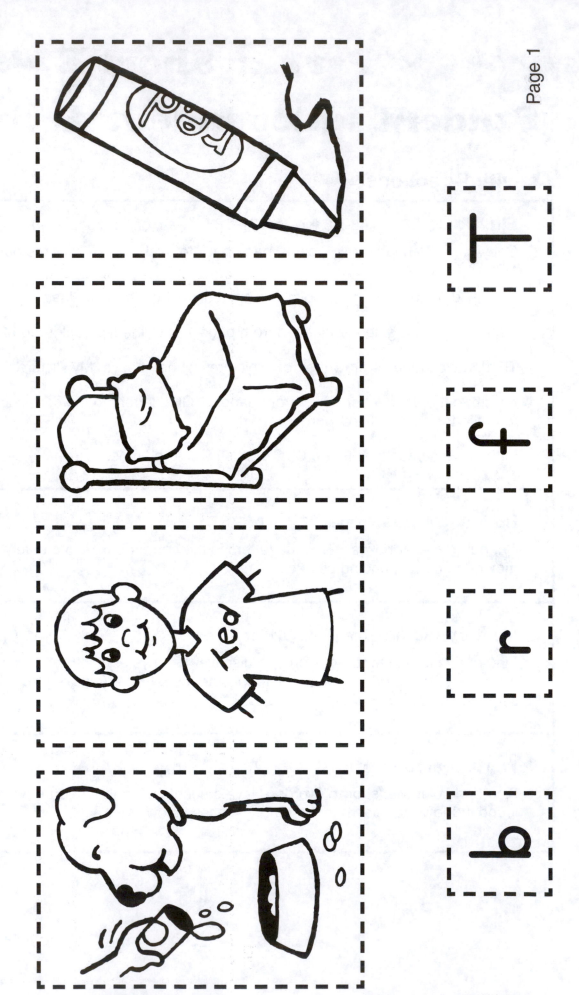

68

fold

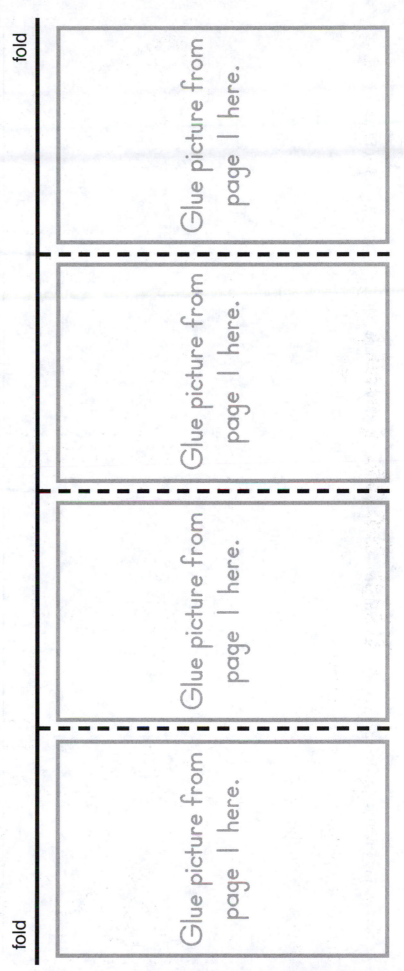

Glue picture from page 1 here.

Glue picture from page 1 here.

Glue picture from page 1 here.

Glue picture from page 1 here.

fold

My Picture

My Picture

My Picture

My Picture

ed

ed

ed

ed

fold

Glue picture from page 1 here.

Glue picture from page 1 here.

Glue picture from page 1 here.

Glue picture from page 1 here.

fold

My Picture

My Picture

My Picture

My Picture

en

en

en

en

Flip Book (–en)

Cut out the pictures and letters below.

Glue them on the flip book.

Flip Book (–et)

Cut out the pictures and letters below.

Glue them on the flip book.

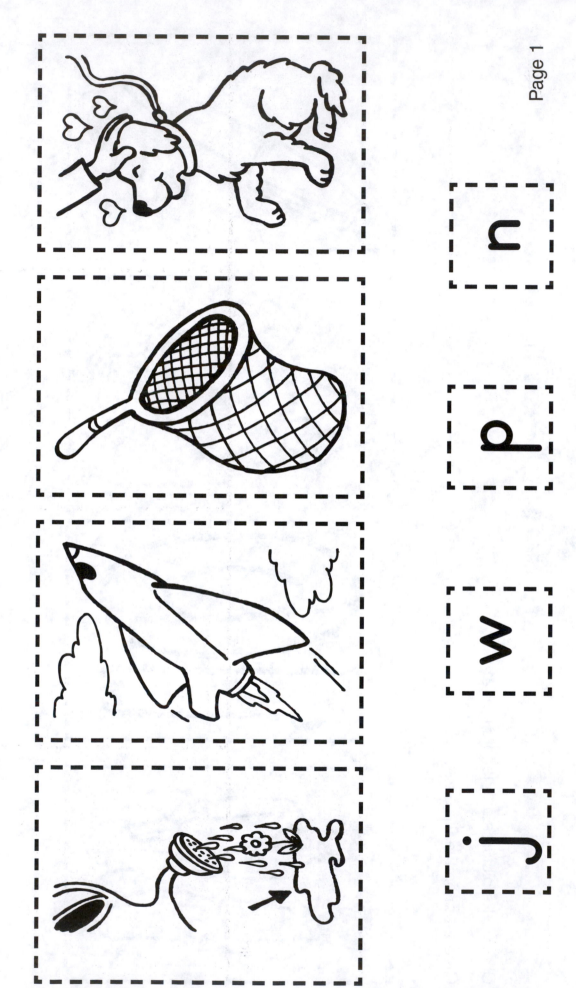

74

fold

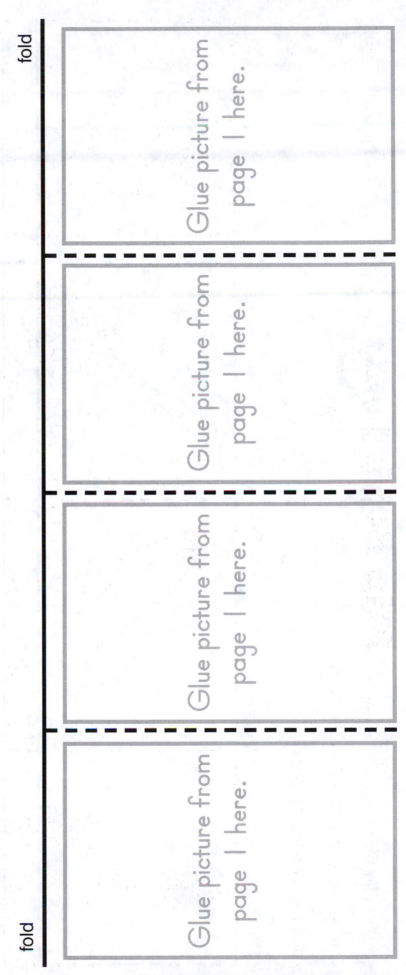

Glue picture from page 1 here.

Glue picture from page 1 here.

Glue picture from page 1 here.

Glue picture from page 1 here.

fold

My Picture

My Picture

My Picture

My Picture

et

et

et

et

Building Words

Cut out the letters below. Glue them in the correct boxes to create words that match the **–ed** pictures.

 # Building Words

Cut out the letters below. Glue them in the correct boxes to create words that match the **–en** pictures.

en

en

en

en

h | p | t | m

Building Words

Cut out the letters below. Glue them in the correct boxes to create words that match the **—et** pictures.

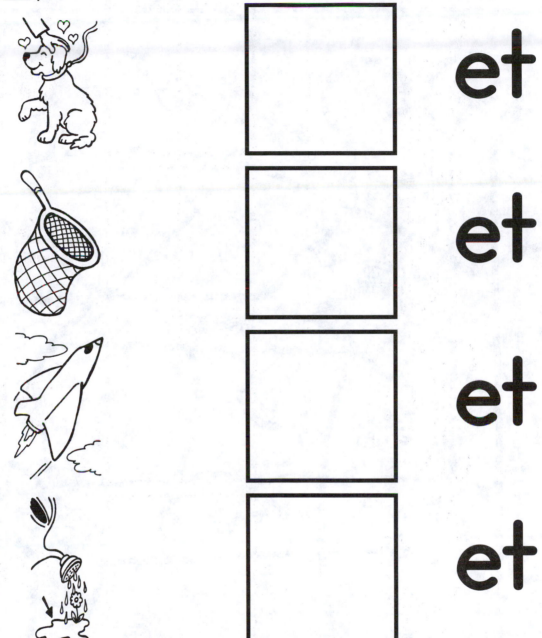

j p w n

Mystery Picture

Color the spaces with **–ed** red to discover the mystery picture. Color the other spaces yellow.

I have a _____ .

Mystery Picture

Color the spaces with **–en** blue to discover the mystery picture. Color the other spaces yellow.

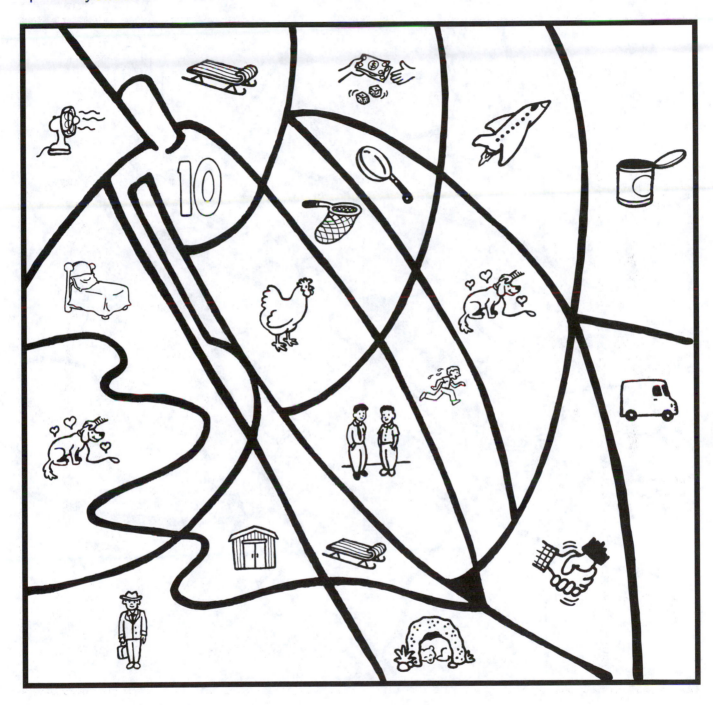

I have a _____ .

Mystery Picture

Color the spaces with __–et__ red to discover the mystery picture. Color the other spaces yellow.

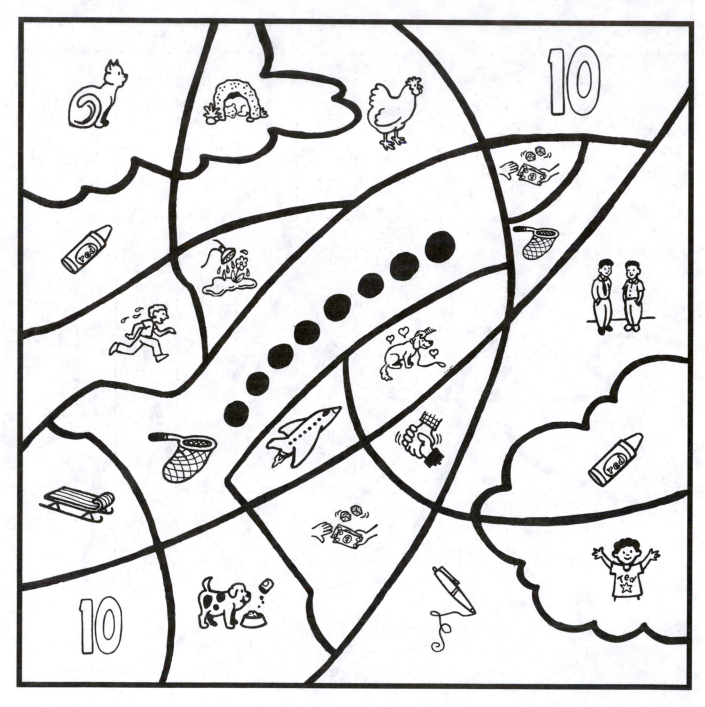

I have a _____ .

Word Search

Find and color the **–ed** words.

fed	red	bed	shed	sled	Ted

c	f	s	h	e	d	p	T
c	m	c	e	u	m	f	e
r	m	f	b	h	z	e	d
a	e	q	e	a	t	h	s
n	n	s	d	u	u	t	l
r	e	d	l	b	g	z	e
h	f	e	d	y	r	a	d

Write the **–ed** words that you have found above.

_____ _____ _____

_____ _____ _____

_____ _____ _____

_____ _____ _____

Word Search

Find and color the __-en__ words.

ten	pen	hen	men	den	Ben

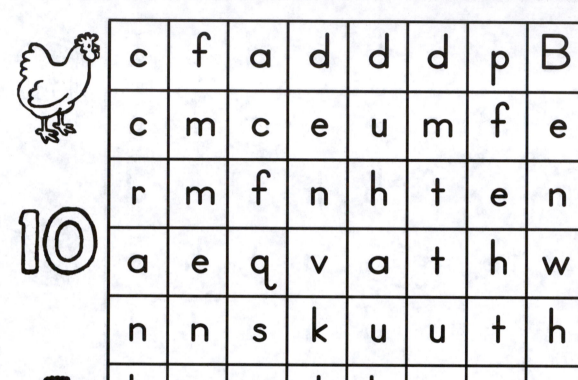

c	f	a	d	d	d	p	B
c	m	c	e	u	m	f	e
r	m	f	n	h	t	e	n
a	e	q	v	a	t	h	w
n	n	s	k	u	u	t	h
h	p	n	l	b	g	z	e
h	p	e	n	y	r	a	n

Write the __-en__ words that you have found above.

_____   _____   _____

- - - - - - - - -   - - - - - - - - -   - - - - - - - - -

_____   _____   _____

- - - - - - - - -   - - - - - - - - -   - - - - - - - - -

_____   _____   _____

- - - - - - - - -   - - - - - - - - -   - - - - - - - - -

Word Search

Find and color the __–et__ words.

pet	wet	jet	met	bet	net

c	f	s	h	e	p	e	t
c	m	c	e	n	e	t	e
r	w	f	b	h	t	c	d
z	e	q	e	a	t	h	s
n	t	s	t	u	u	t	m
j	e	t	l	b	g	z	e
h	f	e	d	y	r	g	t

Write the __–et__ words that you have found above.

_____   _____   _____

- - - - - - - - -   - - - - - - - - -   - - - - - - - - -

_____   _____   _____

- - - - - - - - -   - - - - - - - - -   - - - - - - - - -

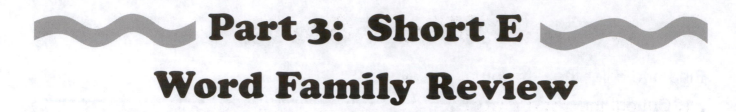

Part 3: Short E
Word Family Review

Activity Directions

Word Sort (pages 87 and 88)

Students will sort CVC words in the correct columns.

(Extension: Have students read the CVC words to classmates.)

Make, Read, and Write CVC Words (page 89)

Students cut out the letter and picture cards on the dashed lines. Students manipulate letter cards to form CVC words. Students then read the words and find the matching pictures. Lastly, students may use blank paper to write the CVC words they have formed. Use plastic baggies or envelopes to store letters and pictures.

Fluency Practice (page 90)

Students read the randomly placed "short e" CVC words from top to bottom. Sand timers may be given to students to time how many words they can read in the given time.

My Own CVC Words (page 91)

Students will write their own "short e" CVC words on the lines provided. They can read and share their words with classmates.

(Note: Students can also cut on the solid lines to make flashcards.)

Making Sentences with CVC Words (pages 92, 93, or 94)

Students will cut out the "short e" CVC words and glue them in the boxes to make sentences. They can use the picture clues. Students should be encouraged to read their sentences aloud.

Word Sort

1. Cut out the **short e** words.

2. Glue each word in the correct column on the following page.

3. Be careful. There are some words that do not belong to the word families.
   Can you find them?

pen	Ted	net	Ben	let
jet	hen	sled	wet	beg
red	met	den	vet	best
ten	fed	pet	bed	get
bet	men	shed	leg	set

-et	-ed	-en

# Make, Read, and Write
CVC Words

Cut on the dashed lines. Make, read, and write **short e** words.

e	t	d	n	p
m	b	n	J	w
h	B	f	r	sh
sl	T			

Fluency Practice

Read → Read → Read → Read → Read →

ten	met	wet	Ted	pet	Ben	bed	pet
shed	den	red	net	den	Ted	hen	bed
fed	sled	pen	hen	sled	net	men	fed
met	bet	jet	jet	bet	men	shed	ten
pet	Ben	bed	pet	red	ten	met	wet
den	Ted	hen	bed	wet	shed	den	red
sled	net	men	fed	pen	fed	sled	pen
red	men	shed	ten	Ben	met	bet	jet

My Own CVC Words (short e)

CVC	CVC	CVC	CVC
CVC	CVC	CVC	CVC

Making Sentences with CVC Words

Cut out the -ed words below. Glue them in the correct boxes to create sentences. Read the sentences aloud.

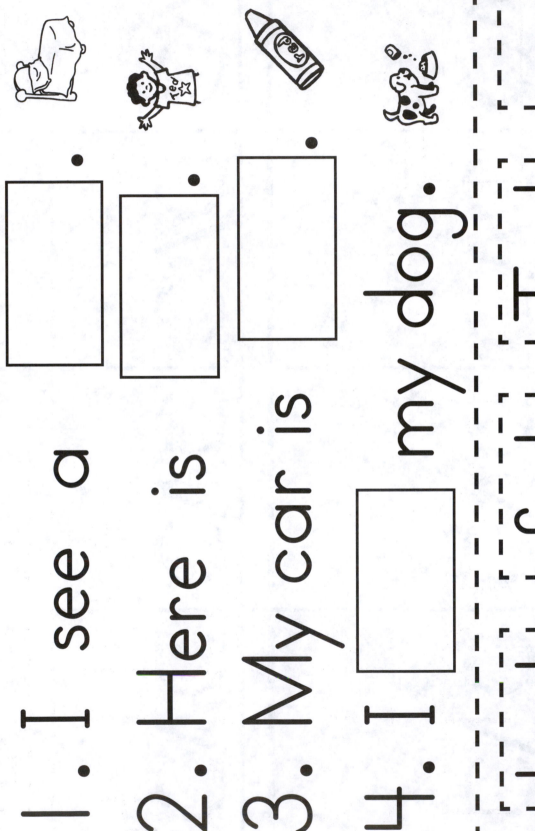

1. I see a ▢ .

2. Here is ▢ .

3. My car is ▢ .

4. I ▢ my dog.

bed

fed

Ted

red

Making Sentences with CVC Words

Cut out the –en words below. Glue them in the correct boxes to create sentences. Read the sentences aloud.

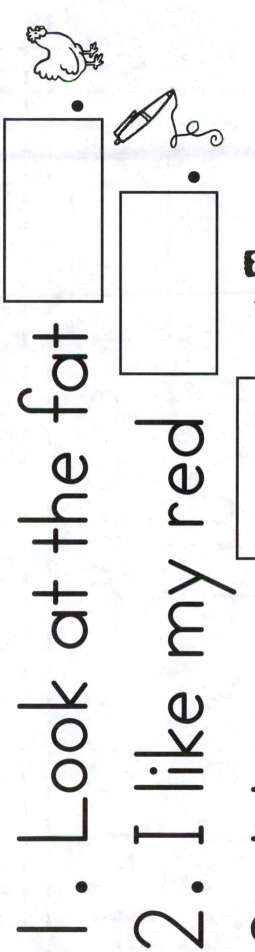

1. Look at the fat ⬜ •

2. I like my red ⬜ •

3. Here is ⬜ •

4. I have ⬜ hats. 10

Ben   hen   ten   pen

Cut out the –et words below. Glue them in the correct boxes to create sentences. Read the sentences aloud.

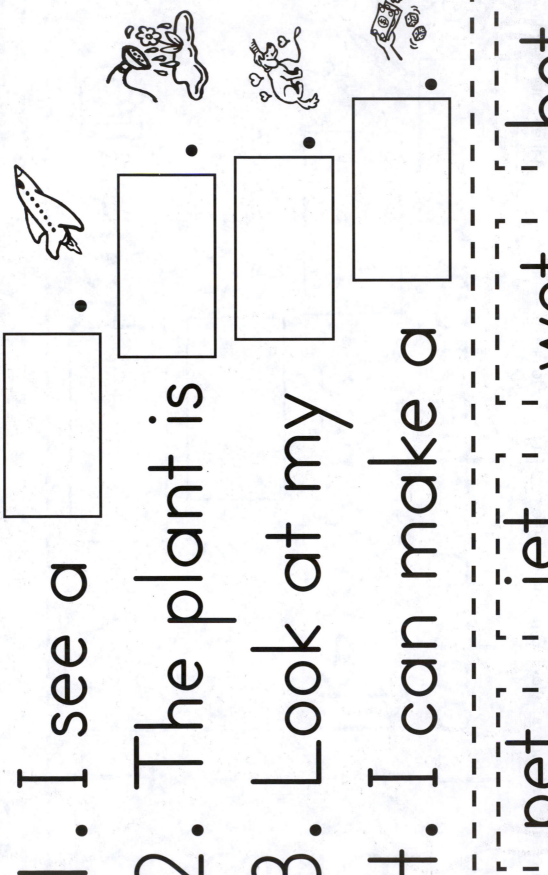

1. I see a [   ] •

2. The plant is [   ] •

3. Look at my [   ] •

4. I can make a [   ] •

pet   jet   wet   bet

Short I

-ig

-ip

-it

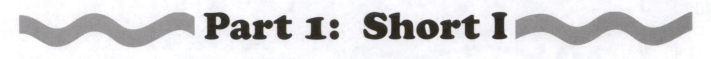

Part 1: Short I
Teacher Support/Home Support

Activity Directions

Flashcards (pages 97 and 98, pages 99 and 100, or pages 101 and 102)

Copy the set of flashcards that you want the students to learn back to back (pages 97 and 98, or pages 99 and 100, or pages 101 and 102). Make sure the cards align properly when copying.

Have students trace and rewrite "short i" words on side A along with reading the words aloud. Side B will allow students to draw their own interpretations of the words. Students will then cut out the cards and place them on a ring for review or use them as a reference.

Letter Slide (pages 103, 104, or 105)

Teacher precuts dashed lines inside picture. Students will cut the strips of letters. Students insert the letter strips to create and manipulate "short i" words.

(*Note:* Students can independently ask other classmates to read the words created with the letter slide.)

Blending Boxes (pages 106, 107, or 108)

First, inform students that they will be building words by listening for beginning, middle, and ending sounds. For example, in *rig*, the *r* can be changed to a *b* to create *big*. Next, the teacher stretches out the word. Both student and teacher repeat the word slowly. Then, the teacher will ask questions to help guide students to develop the sounds to write in the proper boxes. Lastly, students blend the sounds while connecting the dots to show directionality. Students read the words and practice writing them on the line.

Beginning Sound Substitution (pages 109, 110, or 111)

Students cross out the beginning sound to create a new "short i" word. Use the pictures on the left side as a guide. Have students read the words as they create them. The teacher must inform students that they are only substituting the beginning sound to create a new word.

dig

rig

jig

pig

big

fig

rig

dig

pig

jig

fig

big

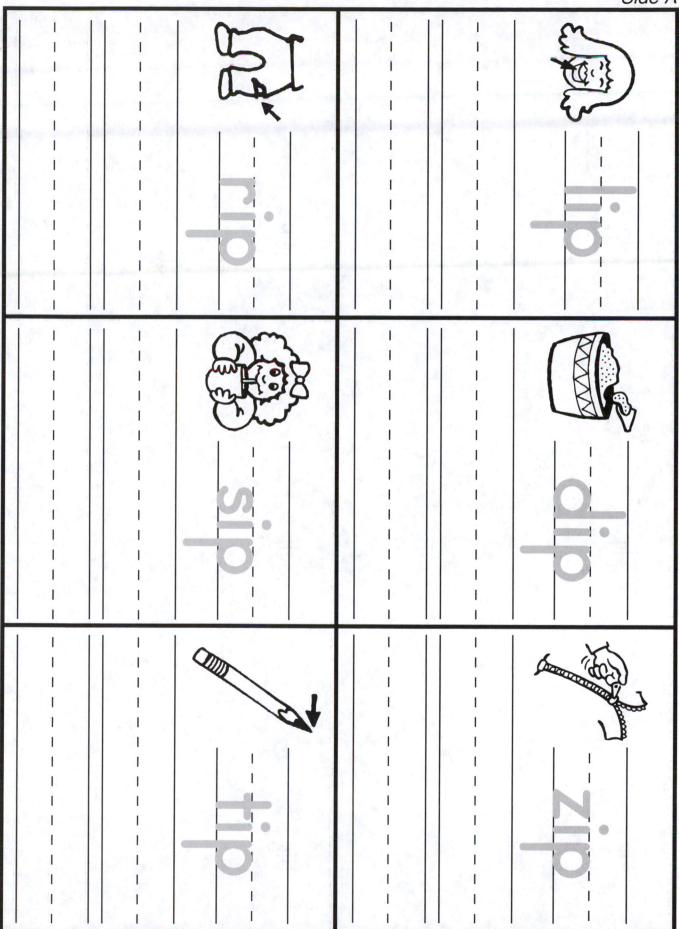

rip

lip

sip

dip

tip

zip

lip

rip

dip

sip

zip

tip

sit

kit

pit

bit

lit

hit

kit

sit

bit

pit

hit

lit

Letter Slide

Cut the strip of letters. Cut the slits on the pig. Insert the strip of letters to create and manipulate the –**ig** words.

b a b a p f j r

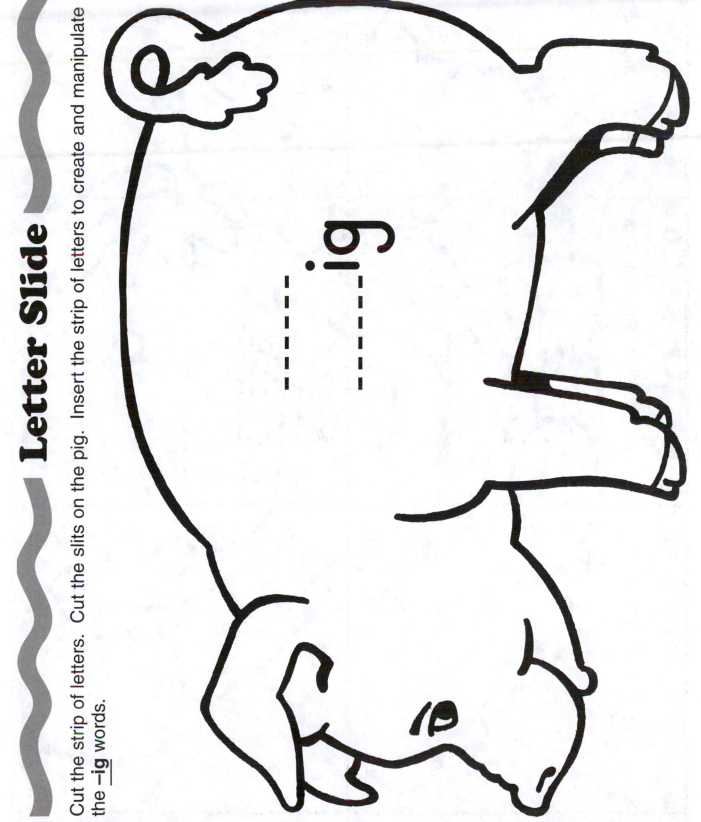

_ig

Letter Slide

Cut the strip of letters. Cut the slits on the cup. Insert the strip of letters to create and manipulate the –**ip** words.

ip

Letter Slide

Cut the strip of letters. Cut the slits on the apple. Insert the strip of letters to create and manipulate the **–it** words.

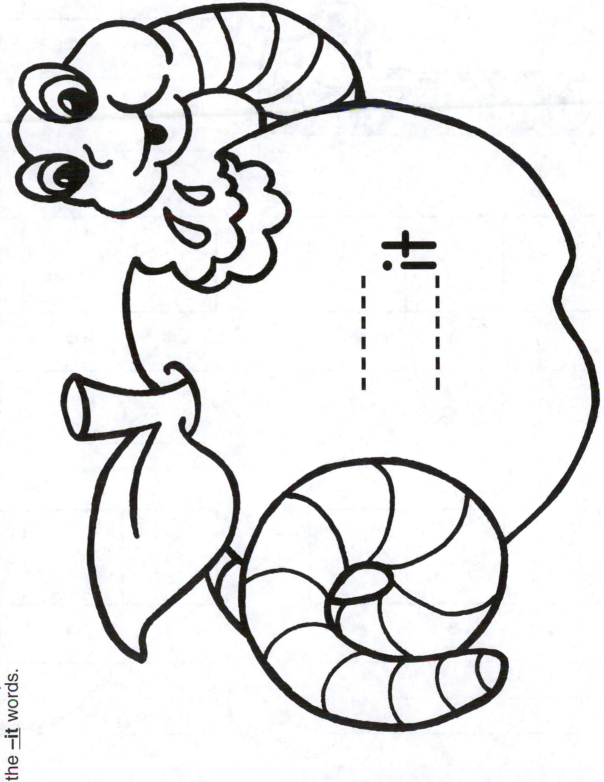

it

Blending Boxes

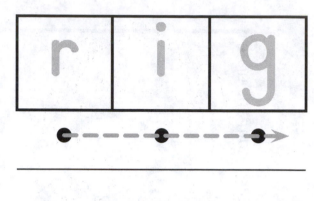

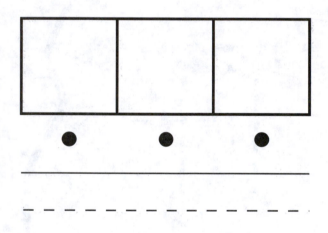

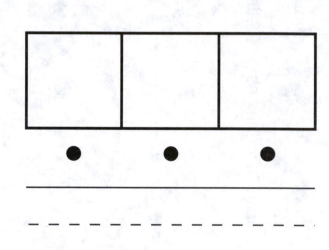

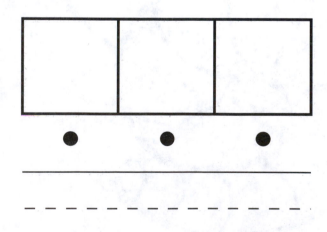

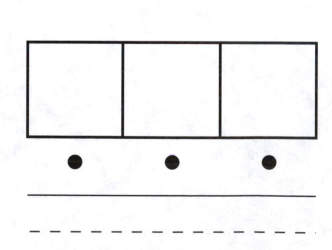

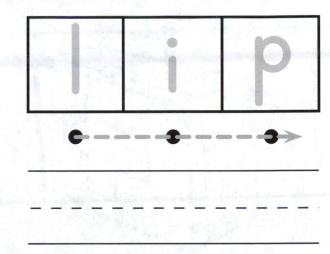

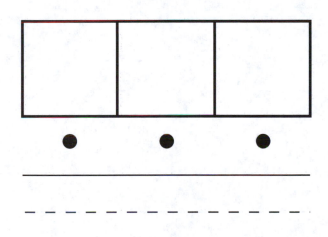

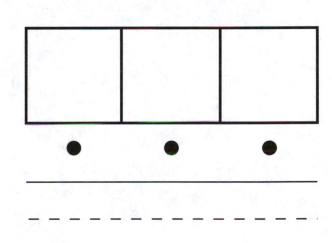

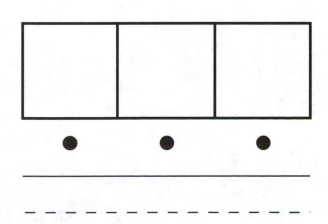

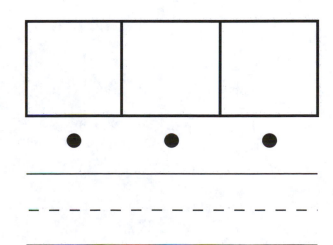

Blending Boxes

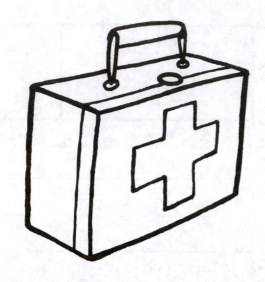

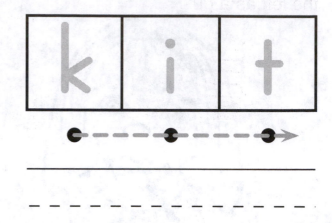

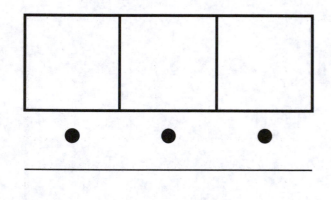

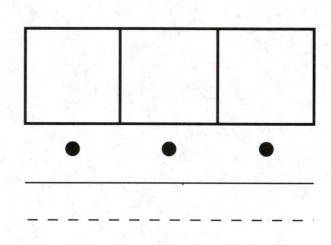

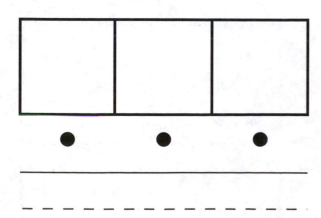

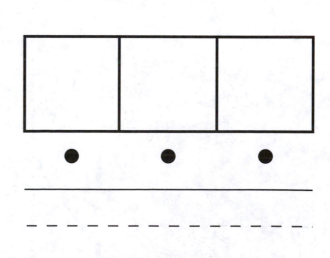

Beginning Sound Substitution

Cross out the beginning sound to create a new **–ig** word. Use the pictures on the left as a guide.

Beginning Sound Substitution

Cross out the beginning sound to create a new **_ip** word. Use the pictures on the left as a guide.

Beginning Sound Substitution

Cross out the beginning sound to create a new **–it** word. Use the pictures on the left as a guide.

Part 2: Short I
Student Independent Activities

Activity Directions

Building Words (pages 113, 114, or 115)

Cut out the letter boxes. Glue the letters in the correct boxes to create words that match the corresponding pictures.

Flip Book (pages 116–118 for *–ig*, 119–121 for *–ip*, or 122–124 for *–it*)

Copy page 2 and the "My Picture" page back to back. Make sure the dashed lines are aligned. Then copy page 1.

First, fold page 2 along the solid line and only cut the dashed lines.

Second, cut and glue the pictures from page 1 onto the flip book (page 2).

Third, have students draw their own pictures where it says "My Picture" in the inside.

Fourth, cut out the letter boxes from page 1. Glue letters to the corresponding pictures to make the correct CVC words.

Fifth, have students write the CVC words two more times.

Mystery Picture (pages 125, 126, or 127)

Find and color the "short i" spaces to discover the mystery picture. Once the mystery picture is discovered, students will then write the "short i" mystery word in the sentence below.

Word Search (pages 128, 129, or 130)

Find and color the "short i" words. Have students write the "short i" words that are found in the word search in the empty spaces below.

Building Words

Cut out the letters below. Glue them in the correct boxes to create words that match the **ig** pictures.

r   p   b   d

Building Words

Cut out the letters below. Glue them in the correct boxes to create words that match the –**ip** pictures.

ip

ip

ip

ip

l   z   r   s

Cut out the letters below. Glue them in the correct boxes to create words that match the **–it** pictures.

Flip Book (-ig)

Cut out the pictures and letters below.

Glue them on the flip book.

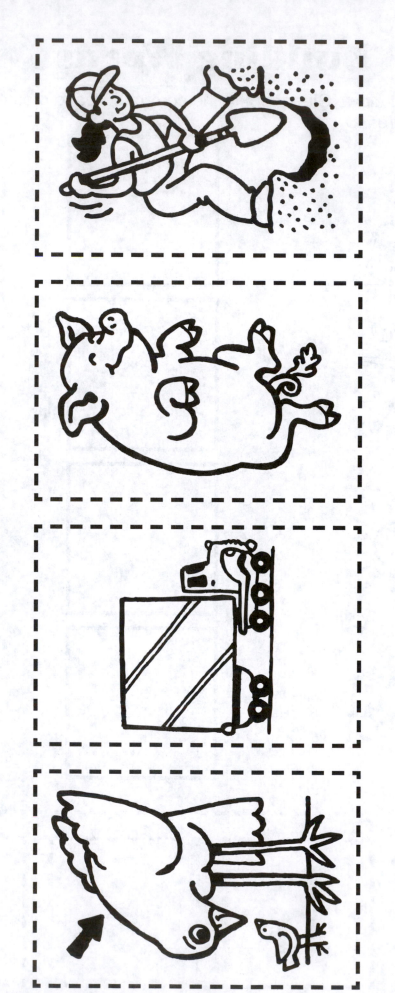

116

fold

Glue picture from page 1 here.

Glue picture from page 1 here.

Glue picture from page 1 here.

Glue picture from page 1 here.

fold

My Picture

My Picture

My Picture

My Picture

ig

ig

ig

ig

fold

Glue picture from page 1 here.

Glue picture from page 1 here.

Glue picture from page 1 here.

Glue picture from page 1 here.

fold

My Picture

My Picture

My Picture

My Picture

ip

ip

ip

ip

Flip Book (-ip)

Cut out the pictures and letters below.

Glue them on the flip book.

Flip Book (–it)

Cut out the pictures and letters below.

Glue them on the flip book.

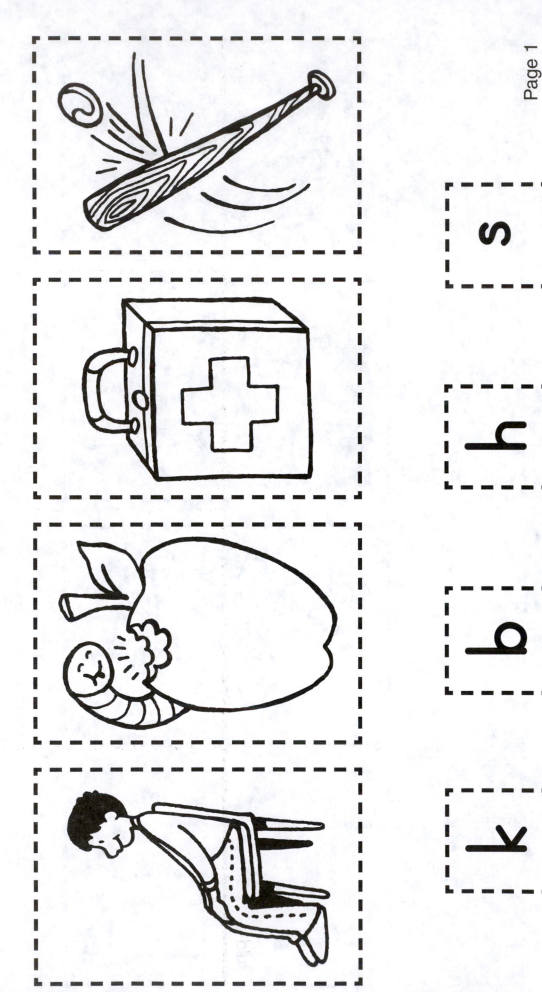

122

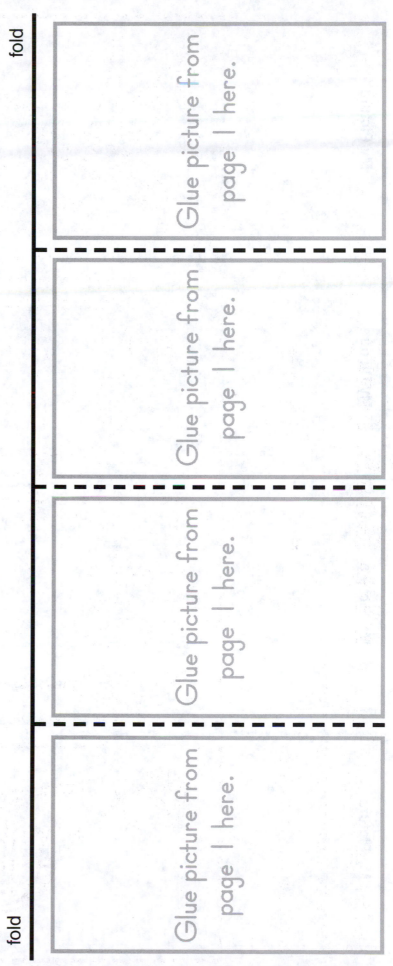

fold

Glue picture from page 1 here.

Glue picture from page 1 here.

Glue picture from page 1 here.

Glue picture from page 1 here.

fold

My Picture

My Picture

My Picture

My Picture

Color the spaces with **–ig** blue to discover the mystery picture. Color the other spaces yellow.

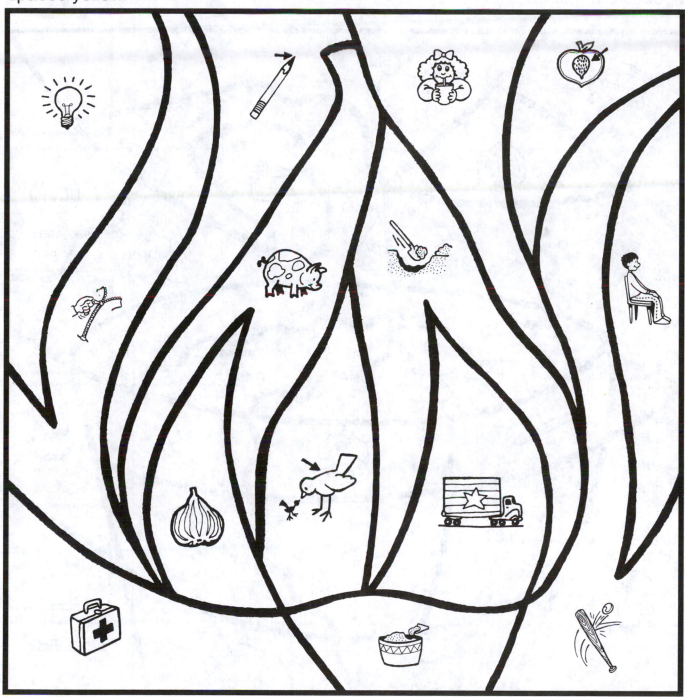

I like the _____ !

Mystery Picture

Color the spaces with **–ip** red to discover the mystery picture. Color the other spaces orange.

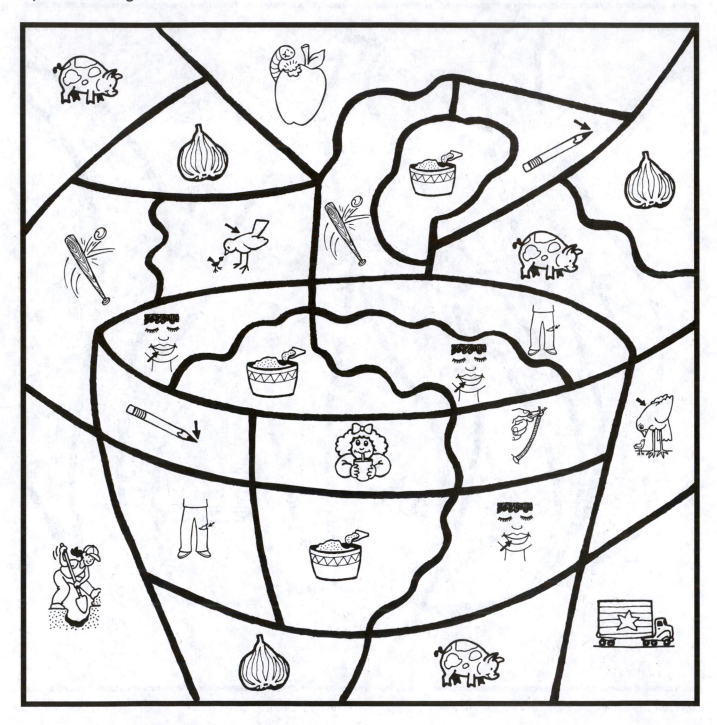

I like the _____!

Mystery Picture

Color the spaces with **–it** red to discover the mystery picture. Color the other spaces yellow.

I see the _____ .

Word Search

Find and color the **–ig** words.

rig	pig	fig	dig	jig	big

c	f	p	d	r	d	p	b
c	m	i	e	u	m	f	i
r	i	g	n	h	j	e	g
a	e	q	v	a	i	h	w
n	n	s	k	u	g	t	d
h	e	n	l	b	g	z	i
h	f	i	g	y	r	a	g

Write the **–ig** words that you have found above.

_____   _____   _____

_____   _____   _____

_____   _____   _____

Word Search

Find and color the **–ip** words.

lip	dip	sip	zip	rip	tip

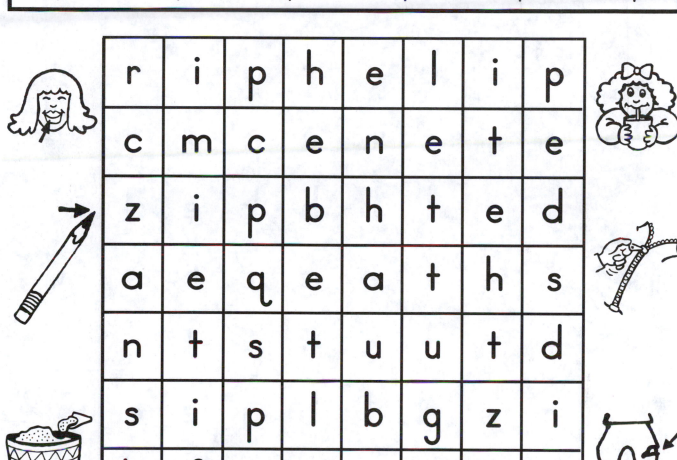

r	i	p	h	e	l	i	p
c	m	c	e	n	e	t	e
z	i	p	b	h	t	e	d
a	e	q	e	a	t	h	s
n	t	s	t	u	u	t	d
s	i	p	l	b	g	z	i
h	f	e	t	i	p	a	p

Write the **–ip** words that you have found above.

_____   _____   _____

_____   _____   _____

_____   _____   _____

Word Search

Find and color the **–it** words.

kit	bit	hit	sit	pit	lit

c	f	b	i	t	d	p	r
c	m	c	e	u	p	i	t
s	m	l	b	h	k	e	d
i	e	i	e	a	i	h	s
t	n	t	d	u	t	t	l
r	e	d	l	b	g	z	e
h	h	i	t	y	r	a	d

Write the **–it** words that you have found above.

_____   _____   _____

_____   _____   _____

_____   _____   _____

_____   _____   _____

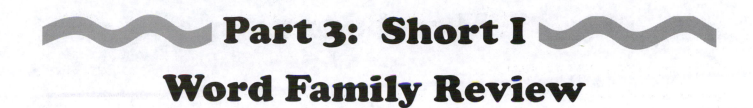

Part 3: Short I
Word Family Review

Activity Directions

Word Sort (pages 132 and 133)

Students will sort CVC words in the correct columns.

(*Extension:* Have students read the CVC words to classmates.)

Make, Read, and Write CVC Words (page 134)

Students cut out the letter and picture cards on the dashed lines. Students manipulate letter cards to form CVC words. Students then read the words and find the matching pictures. Lastly, students may use blank paper to write the CVC words they formed. Use plastic baggies or envelopes to store letters and pictures.

Fluency Practice (page 135)

Students read the randomly placed "short i" CVC words from top to bottom. Sand timers may be given to students to time how many words they can read in the given time.

My Own CVC Words (page 136)

Students will write their own "short i" CVC words on the lines provided. They can read and share their words with classmates.

(*Note:* Students can also cut on the solid lines to make flashcards.)

Making Sentences with CVC Words (pages 137, 138, or 139)

Students will cut out the "short i" CVC words and glue them in the boxes to make sentences. They can use the picture clues. Students should be encouraged to read their sentences aloud.

Word Sort

1. Cut out the **short i** words.

2. Glue each word in the correct column on the following page.

3. Be careful. There are some words that do not belong to the word families. Can you find them?

rig	chin	kit	fin	lip
pig	bit	kid	dip	fig
hit	zip	dig	sit	jig
rip	big	twig	sip	lit
tip	wig	pit	flip	pin

-ig	-it	-ip

Make, Read, and Write CVC Words

Cut on the dashed lines. Make, read, and write **short i** words.

r	p	f	d	j
b	h	s	l	z
t	i	p	k	sh
g				

Fluency Practice

Read

Read	Read	Read	Read
dig	rig	sit	bit
sip	pit	jig	dig
pig			

pit	big	dig	fig
lit	dig	rip	rip
jig			

lit	sit	dip	fig
jig	tip	dig	hit
pit			

fig	zip	rig	big
sip	pit	rip	rip
bit			

sit	sip	pig	lit
tip	rip	bit	zip
dig			

sit	dig	pit	zip
fig	jig	rig	jig
lit			

jig	dip	tip	bit
big	bit	dip	zip
dig			

pig	lit	tip	big
pit	sip	pit	pig
lit			

My Own CVC Words (short i)

CVC	CVC	CVC	CVC
CVC	CVC	CVC	CVC

Making Sentences with CVC Words

Cut out the **-ig** words below. Glue them in the correct boxes to create sentences. Read the sentences aloud.

1. I see a [ ] bird.

2. I like to [ ].

3. I have a fat [ ].

4. I can [ ].

dig   jig   big   pig

Cut out the –ip words below. Glue them in the correct boxes to create sentences. Read the sentences aloud.

1. I can  my jacket.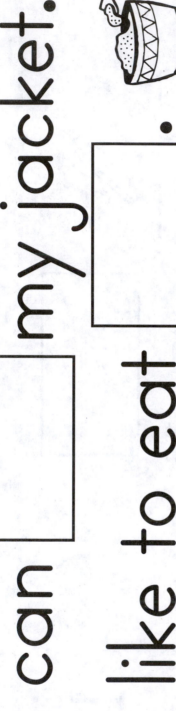

2. I like to eat 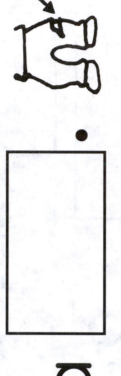.

3. I have a .

4. She can  milk.

dip | rip | sip | zip

Cut out the —it words below. Glue them in the correct boxes to create sentences. Read the sentences aloud.

1. My bat can [ ].

2. I [ ] my lamp.

3. I have a [ ].

4. I can [ ].

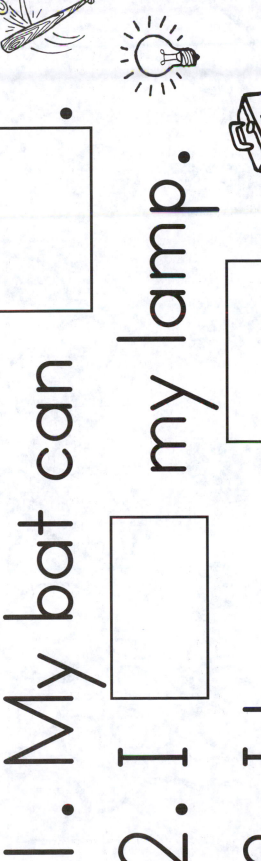

kit   sit   hit   lit

Short O

-og

-op

-ot

Part 1: Short O
Teacher Support/Home Support

Activity Directions

Letter Slide (pages 142, 143, or 144)

Teacher precuts dashed lines inside picture. Students will cut the strips of letters. Students insert the letter strips to create and manipulate "short o" words.

(*Note:* Students can independently ask other classmates to read the words created with the letter slide.)

Flashcards (pages 145–146, 147–148, or 149–150)

Copy the set of flashcards that you want the students to learn back to back (pages 145 and 146, pages 147 and 148, or pages 149 and 150). Make sure the cards align properly when copying.

Have students trace and rewrite "short o" words on side A along with reading the words aloud. Side B will allow students to draw their own interpretations of the words. Students will then cut out the cards and place them on a ring for review or use them as a reference.

Blending Boxes (pages 151, 152, or 153)

First, inform students that they will be building words by listening for beginning, middle, and ending sounds. For example, in *dog*, the *d* can be changed to an *h* to create *hog*. Next, the teacher stretches out the word. Both student and teacher repeat the word slowly. Then, the teacher will ask questions to help guide students to develop the sounds to write in the proper boxes. Lastly, students blend the sounds while connecting the dots to show directionality. Students read the words and practice writing them on the line.

Beginning Sound Substitution (pages 154, 155, or 156)

Students cross out the beginning sound to create a new "short o" word. Use the pictures on the left as a guide. Have students read the words as they create them. The teacher must inform students that they are only substituting the beginning sound to create a new word.

Letter Slide

Cut the strip of letters. Cut the slits on the frog. Insert the strip of letters to create and manipulate the —**og** words.

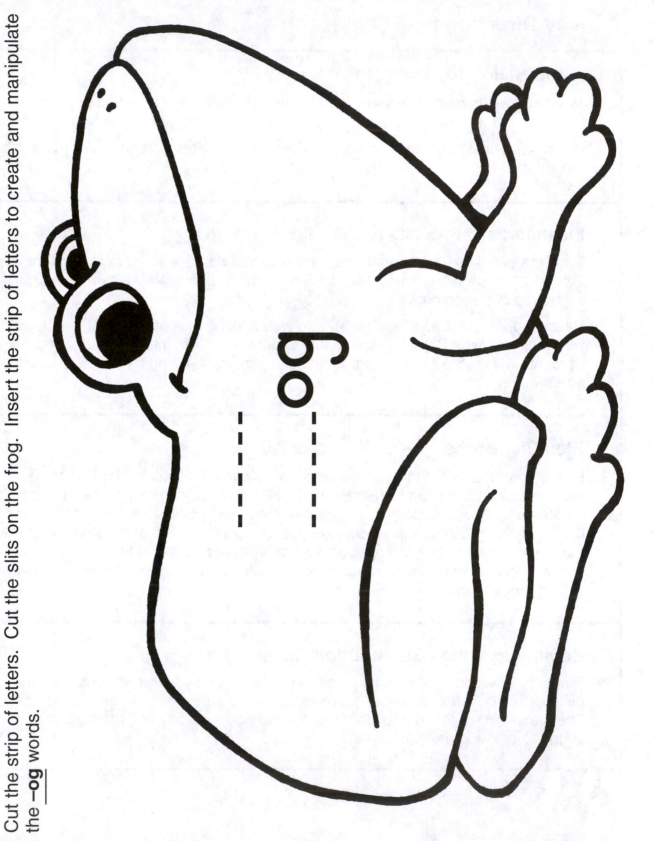

og

d f j l h c f l

Letter Slide

Cut the strip of letters. Cut the slits on the stop sign. Insert the strip of letters to create and manipulate the **–op** words.

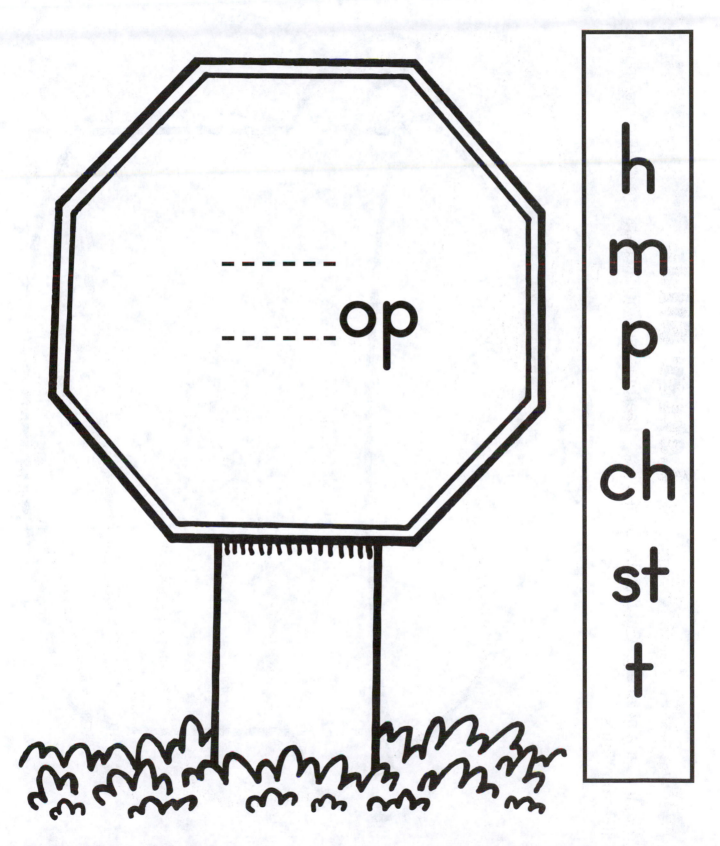

_____
_____op

h
m
p
ch
st
t

Letter Slide

Cut the strip of letters. Cut the slits on the pot. Insert the strip of letters to create and manipulate the —**ot** words.

p
p
d
n
h
sp
c

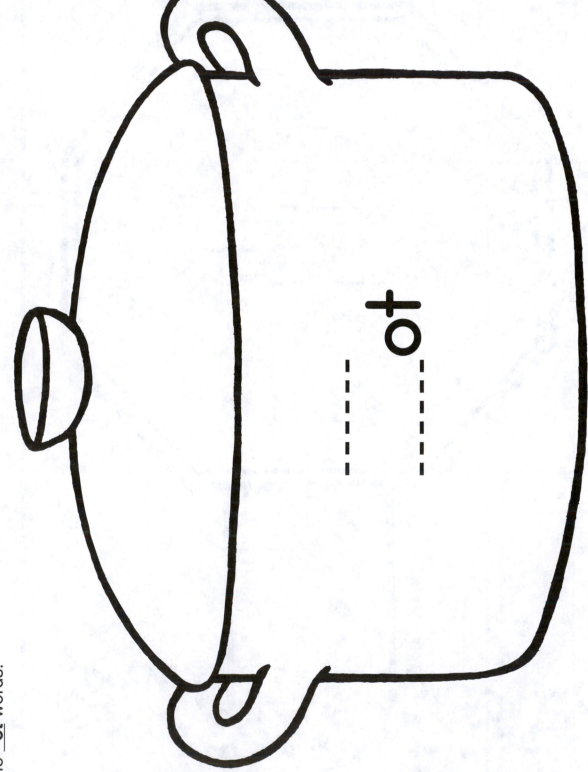

_ot

hog

dog

jog

log

frog

fog

dog

hog

log

jog

fog

frog

stop

pop

hop

top

mop

chop

stop

pop

hop

top

mop

chop

spot

pot

hot

dot

cot

not

pot

spot

dot

hot

not

cot

Blending Boxes

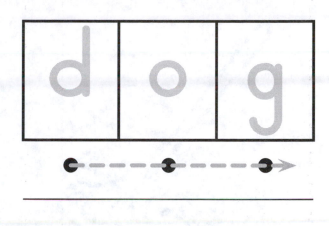

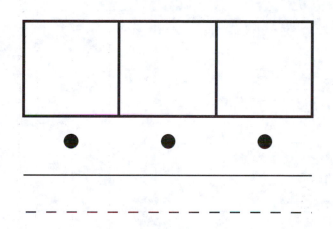

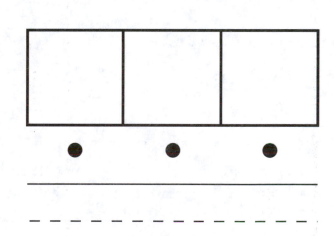

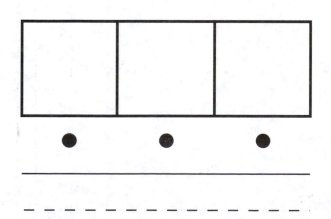

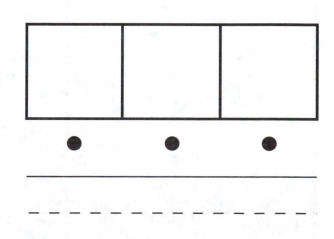

Blending Boxes

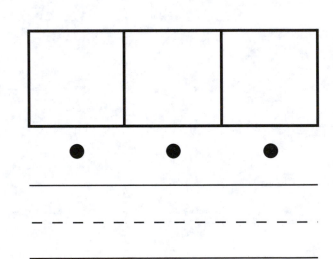

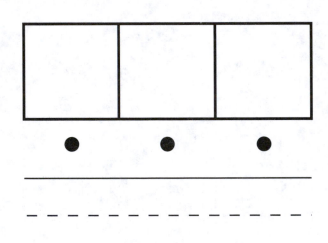

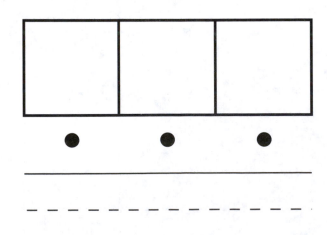

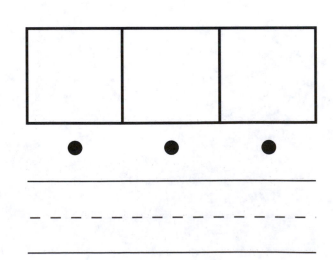

Blending Boxes

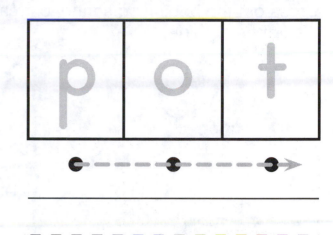

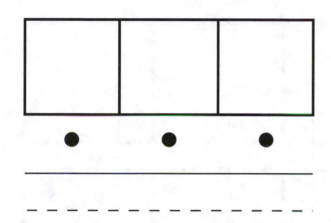

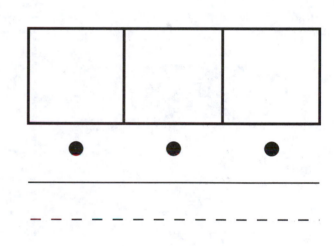

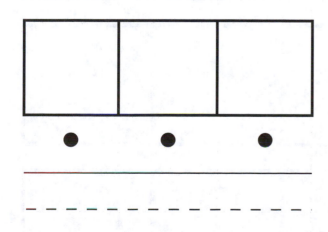

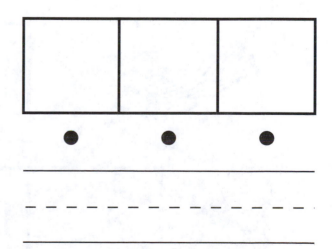

Beginning Sound Substitution

Cross out the beginning sound to create a new **–og** word. Use the pictures on the left as a guide.

Beginning Sound Substitution

Cross out the beginning sound to create a new **–op** word. Use the pictures on the left as a guide.

Beginning Sound Substitution

Cross out the beginning sound to create a new **–ot** word. Use the pictures on the left as a guide.

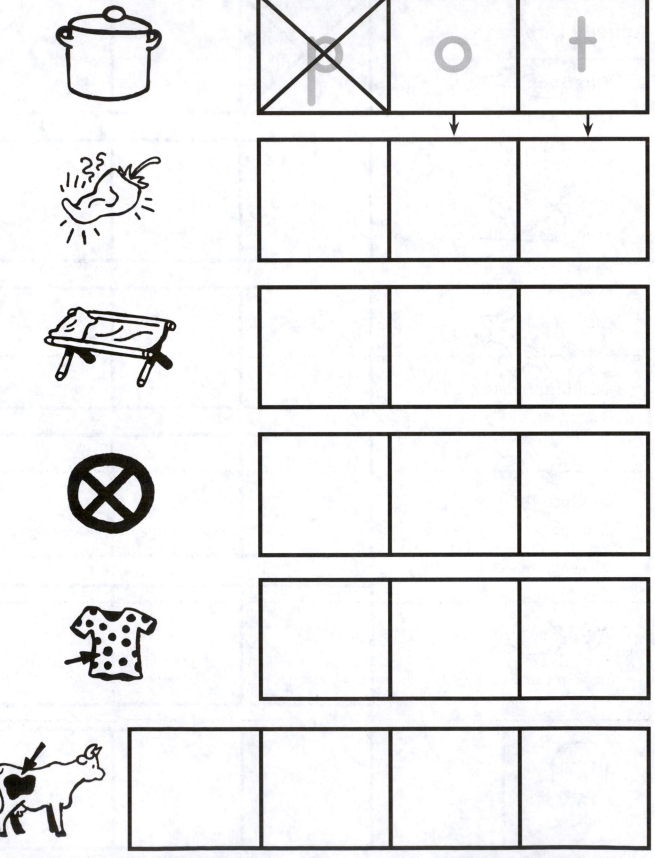

Part 2: Short O
Student Independent Activities

Activity Directions

Flip Book (pages 158–160 for *–og*, 161–163 for *–op*, or 164–166 for *–ot*)

Copy page 2 and the "My Picture" page back to back. Make sure the dashed lines are aligned. Then copy page 1.

First, fold page 2 along the solid line and only cut the dashed lines.

Second, cut and glue the pictures from page 1 onto the flip book (page 2).

Third, have students draw their own pictures where it says "My Picture" in the inside.

Fourth, cut out the letter boxes from page 1. Glue the letters to the corresponding pictures to make the correct CVC words.

Fifth, have students write the CVC words two more times.

Building Words (pages 167, 168, or 169)

Cut out the letter boxes. Glue the letters in the correct boxes to create words that match the corresponding pictures.

Mystery Picture (pages 170, 171, or 172)

Find and color the "short o" words to discover the mystery picture. Once the mystery picture is discovered, students will then write the "short o" mystery word in the sentence below.

Word Search (pages 173, 174, or 175)

Find and color the "short o" words. Have students write the "short o" words that are found in the word search in the empty spaces at the bottom of the page.

Flip Book (–og)

Cut out the pictures and letters below.

Glue them on the flip book.

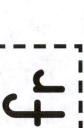

fold

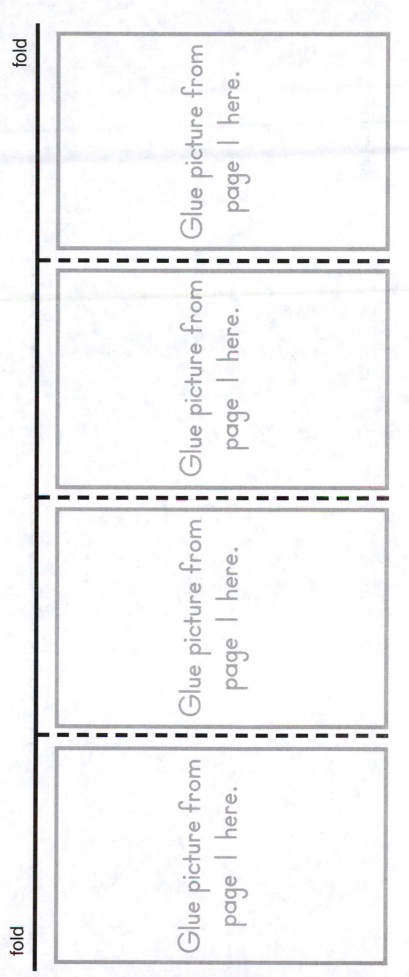

Glue picture from page 1 here.

Glue picture from page 1 here.

Glue picture from page 1 here.

Glue picture from page 1 here.

fold

#2076 Word Family Activities: Short Vowels

My Picture

My Picture

My Picture

My Picture

og

og

og

og

fold

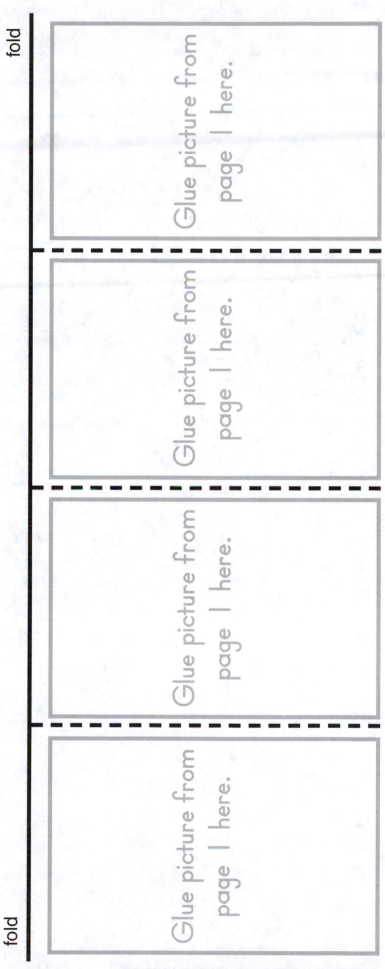

Glue picture from page 1 here.

Glue picture from page 1 here.

Glue picture from page 1 here.

Glue picture from page 1 here.

fold

My Picture

My Picture

My Picture

My Picture

op

op

op

op

Flip Book (–op)

Cut out the pictures and letters below.

Glue them on the flip book.

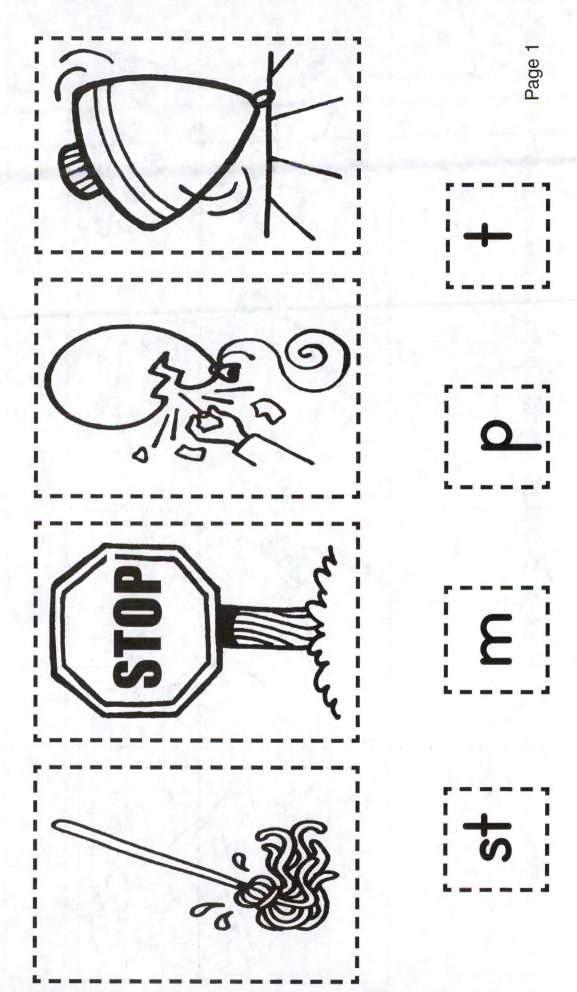

t

p

m

st

Flip Book (–ot)

Cut out the pictures and letters below.

Glue them on the flip book.

c

h

p

d

fold

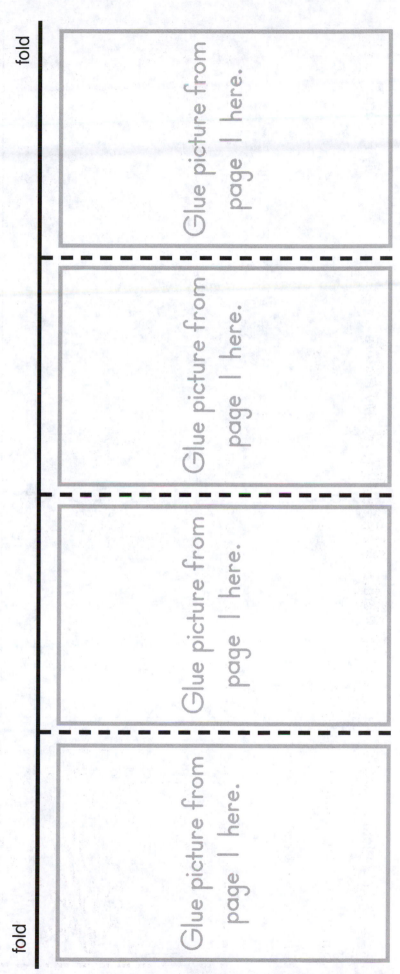

Glue picture from page 1 here.

Glue picture from page 1 here.

Glue picture from page 1 here.

Glue picture from page 1 here.

fold

My Picture

My Picture

My Picture

My Picture

ot

ot

ot

ot

Building Words

Cut out the letters below. Glue them in the correct boxes to create words that match the **–og** pictures.

Building Words

Cut out the letters below. Glue them in the correct boxes to create words that match the **–op** pictures.

op

op

op

op

h   m   p   t

Building Words

Cut out the letters below. Glue them in the correct boxes to create words that match the **–ot** pictures.

ot

ot

ot

ot

d   c   p   h

Mystery Picture

Color the spaces with **–og** pictures brown to discover the mystery picture. Color the other spaces blue.

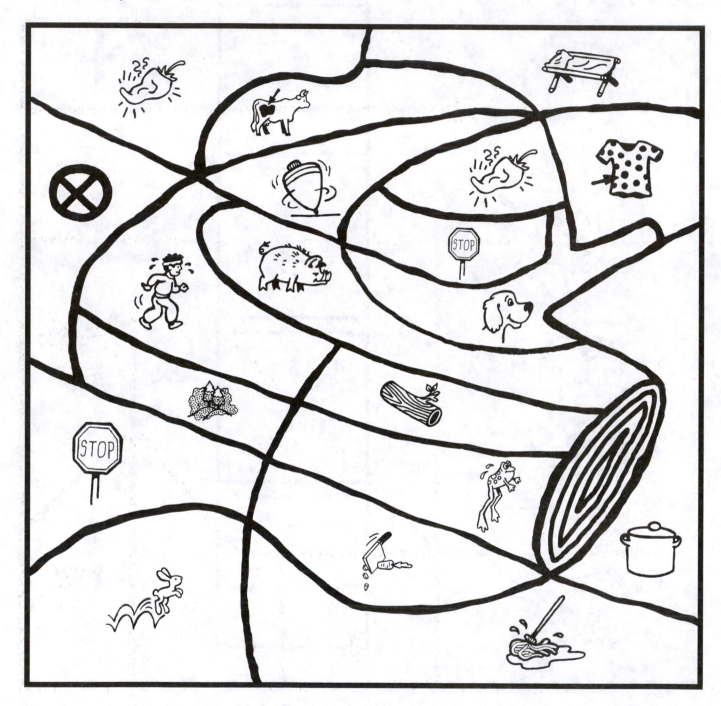

Look at the _____ .

Mystery Picture

Color the spaces with **–op** red to discover the mystery picture. Color the other spaces yellow.

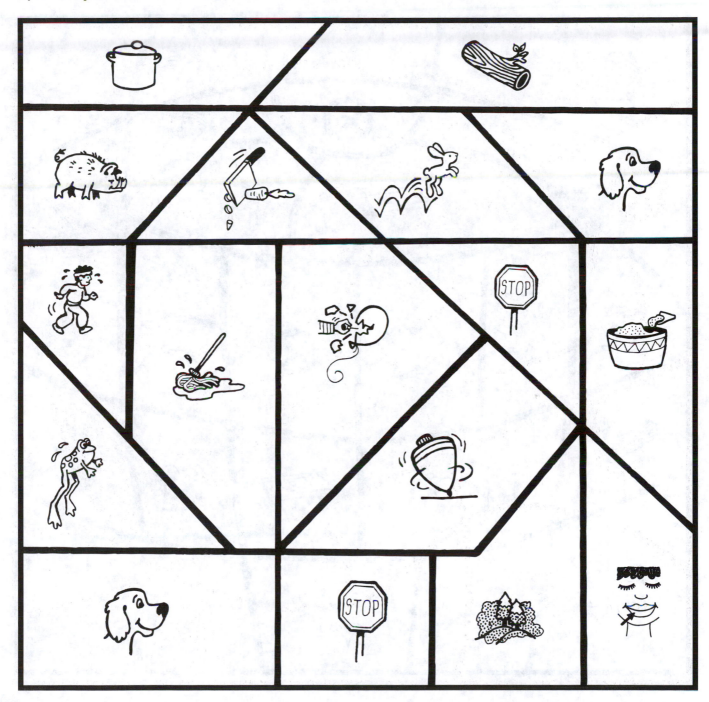

We must _____ !

Mystery Picture

Color the spaces with **–ot** pictures gray to discover the mystery picture. Color the other spaces green.

Look at the _____ .

Word Search

Find and color the **–og** words.

dog	log	fog	hog	jog	frog

l	f	p	d	r	d	p	h
o	m	i	e	u	m	f	o
g	i	m	n	d	o	g	g
a	e	o	v	f	i	h	w
f	n	g	d	r	g	t	j
o	e	n	l	o	g	z	i
g	f	i	g	g	j	o	g

Write the **–og** words that you have found above.

_____ _____ _____

_____ _____ _____

_____ _____ _____

Word Search

Find and color the **-op** words.

stop	hop	mop	pop	top	chop

c	h	o	p	s	t	o	p
c	m	c	e	n	e	t	e
z	i	p	t	h	t	e	h
a	e	q	o	a	t	h	o
n	t	s	p	u	u	t	p
p	o	p	l	b	g	z	i
h	f	e	t	i	m	o	p

Write the **-op** words that you have found above.

_____   _____   _____

_____   _____   _____

_____   _____   _____

_____   _____   _____

Word Search

Find and color the **–ot** words.

pot	dot	not	spot	hot	cot

c	f	c	o	t	d	p	g
c	m	c	e	u	p	o	f
s	m	d	o	t	k	t	e
i	e	i	e	s	i	h	h
t	n	t	d	p	t	t	o
r	e	d	l	o	g	z	t
n	o	t	b	t	r	a	d

Write the **–ot** words that you have found above.

_____   _____   _____

_____   _____   _____

_____   _____   _____

_____   _____   _____

Part 3: Short O
Word Family Review

Activity Directions

Word Sort (pages 177 and 178)

Students will sort CVC words in the correct columns.

(*Extension:* Have students read the CVC words to classmates.)

Make, Read, and Write CVC Words (page 179)

Students cut out the letter and picture cards on the dashed lines. Students manipulate letter cards to form CVC words. Students then read the words and find the matching pictures. Lastly, students may use blank paper to write the CVC words they have formed. Use plastic baggies or envelopes to store letters and pictures.

Fluency Practice (page 180)

Students read the randomly placed "short o" CVC words from top to bottom. Sand timers may be given to students to time how many words they can read in the given time.

My Own CVC Words (page 181)

Students will write their own "short o" CVC words on lines provided. They can read and share their words with classmates.

(*Note:* Students can also cut on the solid lines to make flashcards.)

Making Sentences with CVC Words (pages 182, 183, or 184)

Students will cut out the "short o" CVC words and glue them in the boxes to make sentences. They can use the picture clues. Students should be encouraged to read their sentences aloud.

 # Word Sort

1. Cut out the **short o** words.

2. Glue each word in the correct column on the following page.

3. Be careful. There are some words that do not belong to the word families. Can you find them?

got	dot	hog	top	drop
dog	pop	mop	frog	hot
pot	fog	fox	lot	chop
stop	not	jog	mom	shop
log	hop	spot	cot	box

-og	-ot	-op

 # Make, Read, and Write CVC Words

Cut on the dashed lines. Make, read, and write **short o** words.

g	l	f	h	j
fr	p	d	n	sp
c	st	m	p	t
ch	o			

Fluency Practice

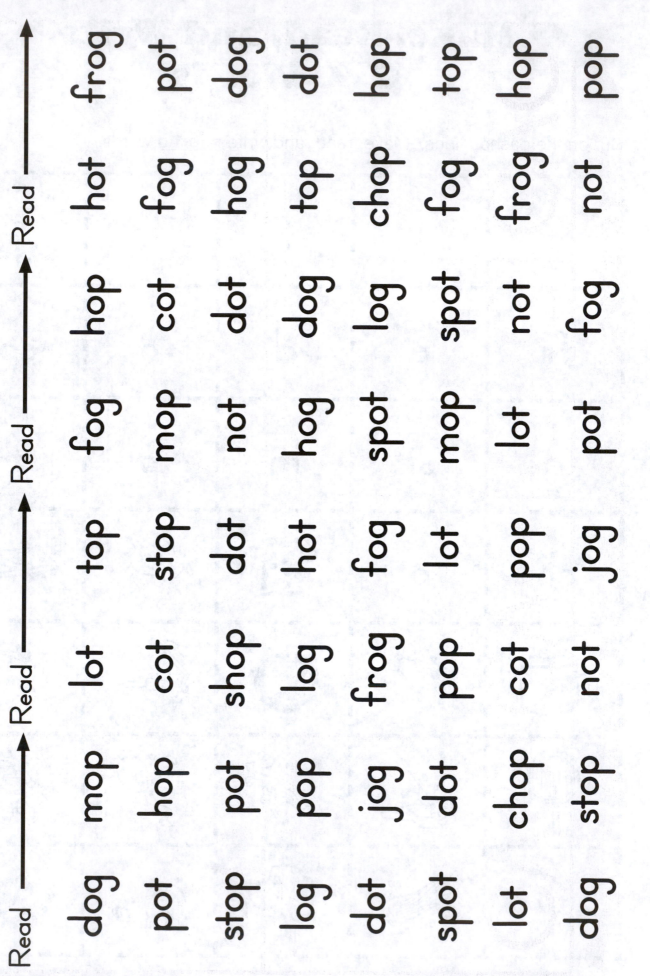

Read	Read	Read	Read	Read	Read
frog	hot	hop	fog	top	lot	mop	dog
pot	fog	cot	mop	stop	cot	hop	pot
dog	hog	dot	not	dot	shop	pot	stop
dot	top	dog	hog	hot	log	pop	log
hop	chop	log	spot	fog	frog	jog	dot
top	fog	spot	mop	lot	pop	dot	spot
hop	frog	not	lot	pop	cot	chop	lot
pop	not	fog	pot	jog	not	stop	dog

My Own CVC Words (short o)

CVC	CVC	CVC	CVC
CVC	CVC	CVC	CVC

Cut out the —og words below. Glue them in the correct boxes to create sentences. Read the sentences aloud.

1. I have a big  ▢

2. I like my green ▢

3. Look at the ▢

4. She can ▢

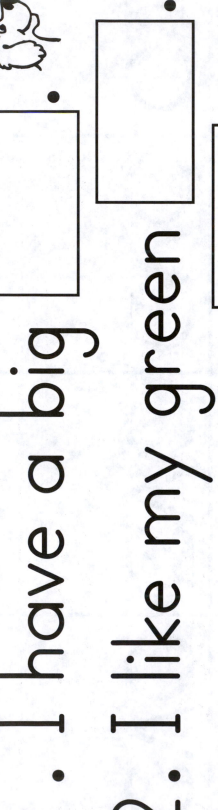

frog

dog

fog

jog

Making Sentences with CVC Words

Cut out the –**op** words below. Glue them in the correct boxes to create sentences. Read the sentences aloud.

1. The [____] sign is red.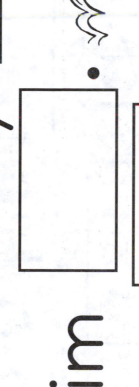

2. I play with my [____].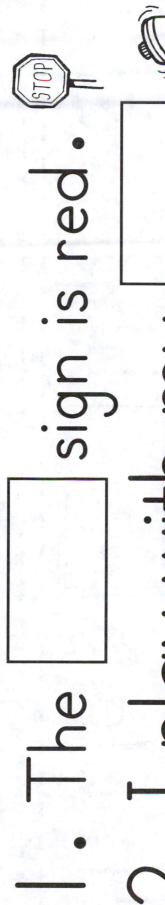

3. See him [____].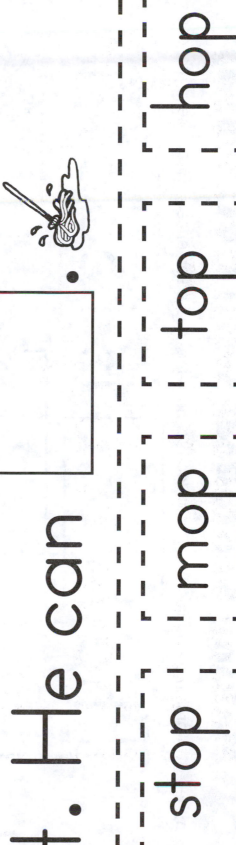

4. He can [____].

stop | mop | top | hop

Making Sentences with CVC Words

Cut out the **-ot** words below. Glue them in the correct boxes to create sentences. Read the sentences aloud.

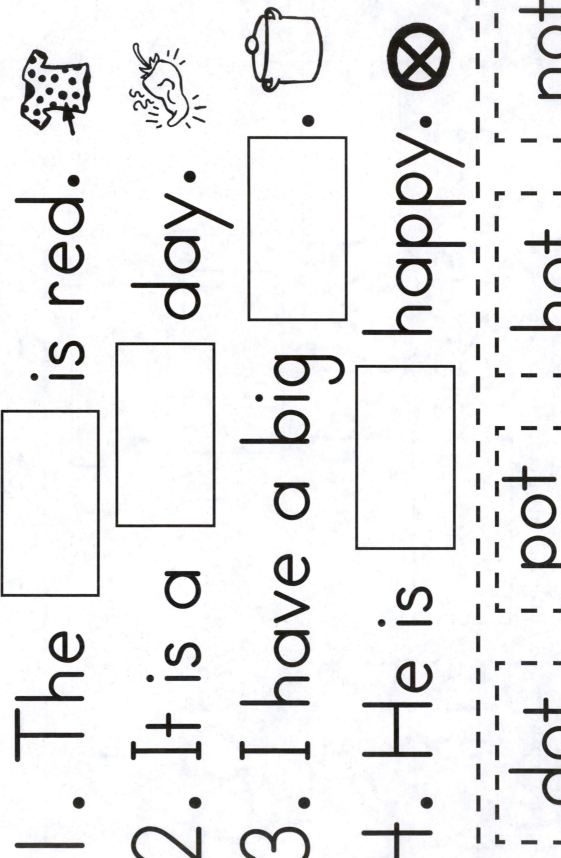

1. The [ ] is red.

2. It is a [ ] day.

3. I have a big [ ].

4. He is [ ] happy.

dot | pot | hot | not

Short U

-ug

-un

-ut

Part 1: Short U
Teacher Support/Home Support

Activity Directions

Flashcards (pages 187 and 188, pages 189 and 190, or pages 191 and 192)

Copy the set of flashcards that you want the students to learn back to back (pages 187 and 188, pages 189 and 190, or pages 191 and 192). Make sure the cards align properly when copying.

Have students trace and rewrite "short u" words on side A along with reading the words aloud. Side B will allow students to draw their own interpretations of the words. Students will then cut out the cards and place them on a ring for review or use them as a reference.

Letter Slide (page 193, 194, or 195)

Teacher precuts dashed lines inside picture. Students will cut the strips of letters. Students insert the letter strips to create and manipulate "short u" words.

(*Note:* Students can independently ask other classmates to read the words created with the letter slide.)

Blending Boxes (page 196, 197, or 198)

First, inform students that they will be building words by listening for beginning, middle, and ending sounds. For example, in *bug*, the *b* can be changed to *d* to create *dug*. Next, the teacher stretches out the word. Both student and teacher repeat the word slowly. Then, the teacher will ask questions to help guide students to develop the sounds to write in the proper boxes. Lastly, students blend the sounds while connecting the dots to show directionality. Students read the words and practice writing them on the line.

Beginning Sound Substitution (page 199, 200, or 201)

Students cross out the beginning sound to create a new "short u" word. Use the pictures on the left as a guide. Have students read the words as they create them. The teacher must inform students that they are only substituting the beginning sound to create a new word.

jug

rug

dug

hug

bug

mug

rug

jug

hug

pug

mug

bug

bun

run

sun

fun

gun

fun

bun

run

sun

nun

fun

gun

gut

hut

nut

cut

shut

rut

hut

gut

cut

nut

rut

shut

Letter Slide

Cut the strip of letters. Cut the slits on the bug. Insert the strip of letters to create and manipulate the **–ug** words.

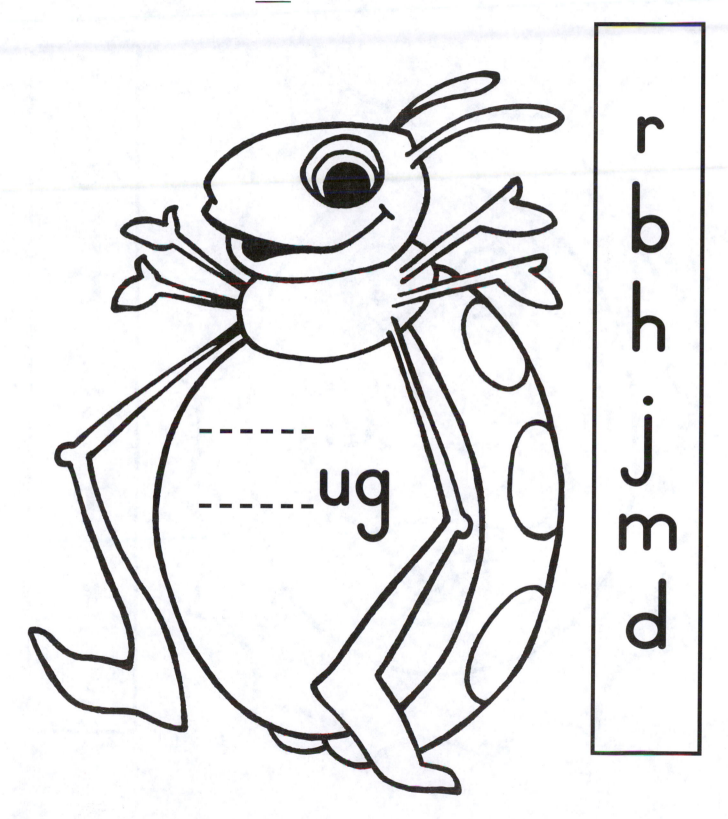

_____

_____ug

r
b
h
j
m
d

Letter Slide

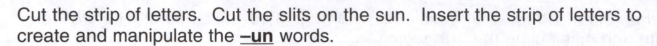

Cut the strip of letters. Cut the slits on the sun. Insert the strip of letters to create and manipulate the **–un** words.

Letter Slide

Cut the strip of letters. Cut the slits on the hut. Insert the strip of letters to create and manipulate the **–ut** words.

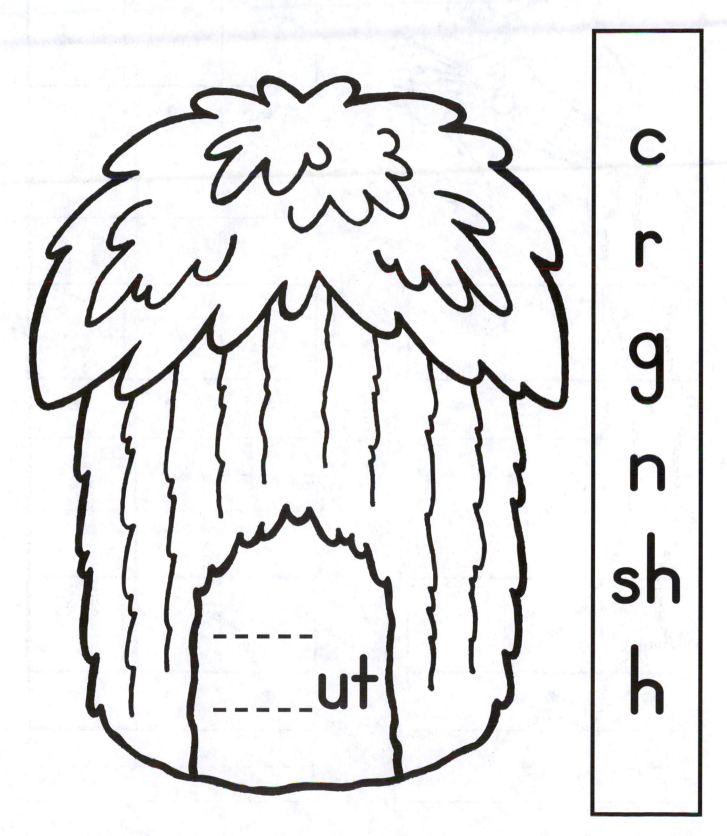

_____
_____ut

c
r
g
n
sh
h

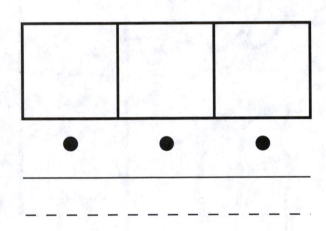
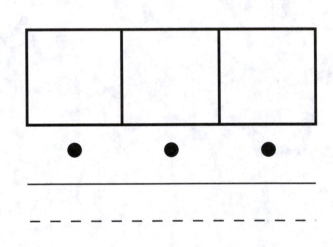
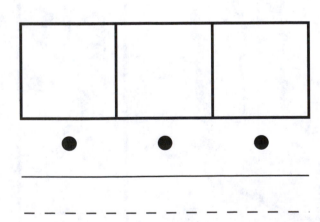

Blending Boxes

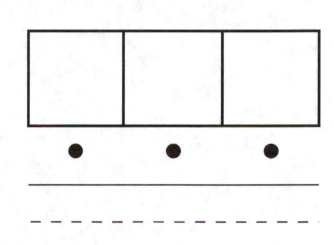

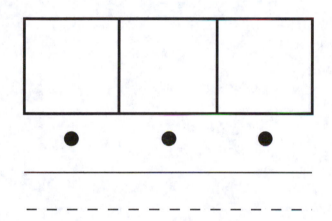

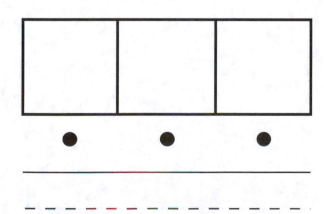

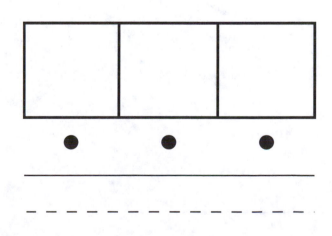

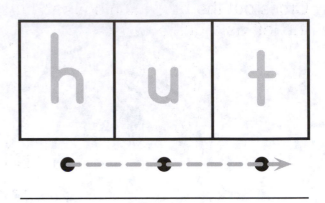

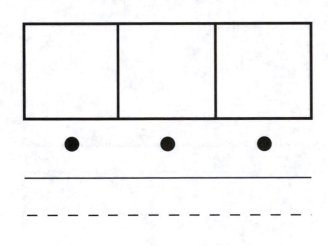

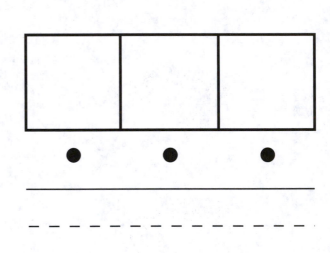

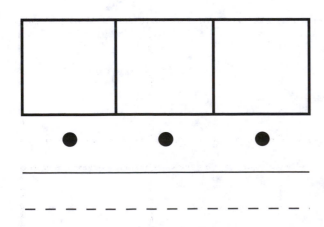

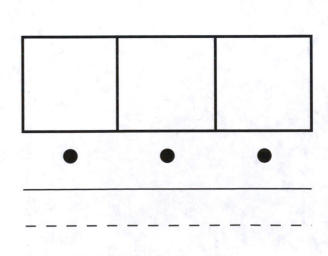

Beginning Sound Substitution

Cross out the beginning sound to create a new **–ug** word. Use the pictures on the left as a guide.

Beginning Sound Substitution

Cross out the beginning sound to create a new **–un** word. Use the pictures on the left as a guide.

Beginning Sound Substitution

Cross out the beginning sound to create a new **–ut** word. Use the pictures on the left as a guide.

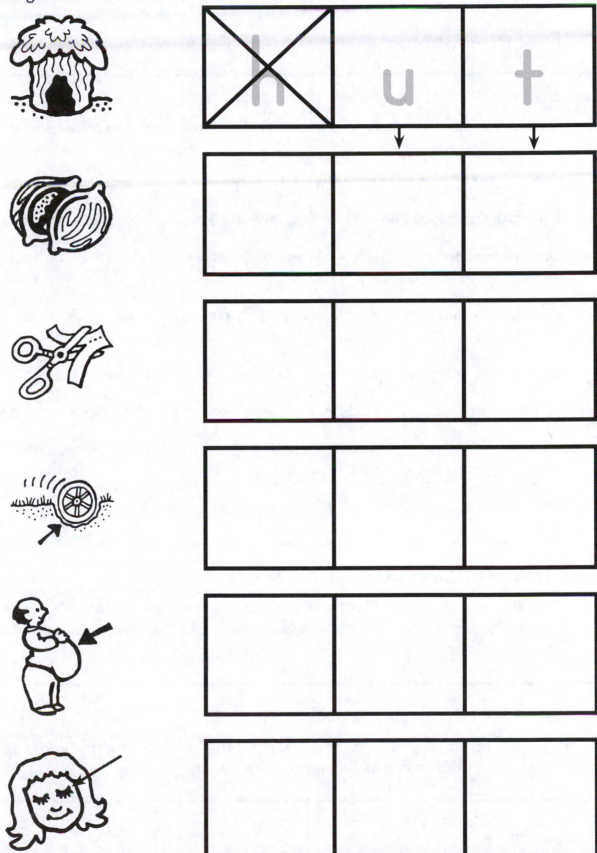

Part 2: Short U
Student Independent Activities

Activity Directions

Building Words (pages 203, 204, or 205)

Cut out the letter boxes. Glue the letters in the correct boxes to create words that match the corresponding pictures.

Flip Book (pages 206–208 for *–ug*, 209–211 for *–un*, or 212–214 for *–ut*)

Copy page 2 and the "My Picture" page back to back. Make sure the dashed lines are aligned. Then copy page 1.

First, fold page 2 along the solid line and only cut the lines dashed lines that are dashes.

Second, cut and glue the pictures from page 1 onto the flip book (page 2).

Third, have students draw their own pictures where it says "My Picture" in the inside.

Fourth, cut out the letter boxes from page 1. Glue letters to the corresponding pictures to make the correct CVC words.

Fifth, have students write the CVC words two more times.

Mystery Picture (pages 215, 216, or 217)

Find and color the "short u" pictures to discover the mystery picture. Once the mystery picture is discovered, students will then write the "short u" mystery word in the sentence below.

Word Search (pages 218, 219, or 220)

Find and color the "short u" words. Have students write the "short u" words that are found in the word search in the empty spaces below.

Building Words

Cut out the letters below. Glue them in the correct boxes to create words that match the **–ug** pictures.

Building Words

Cut out the letters below. Glue them in the correct boxes to create words that match the **–un** pictures.

un

un

un

un

s   b   r   f

Building Words

Cut out the letters below. Glue them in the correct boxes to create words that match the **–ut** pictures.

ut

ut

ut

ut

h   c   sh   n

Flip Book (-ug)

Cut out the pictures and letters below.

Glue them on the flip book.

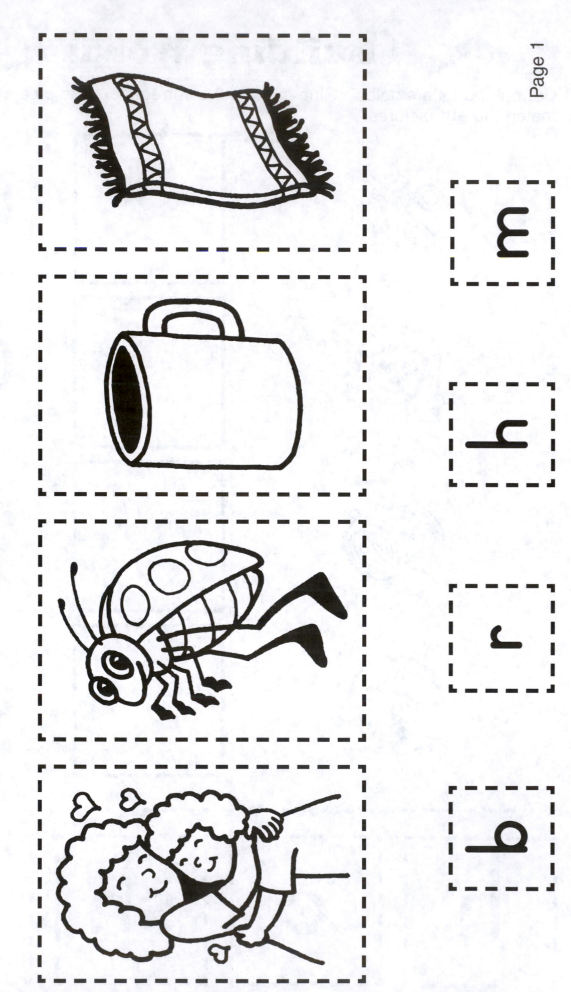

206 ©Teacher Created Resources, Inc.

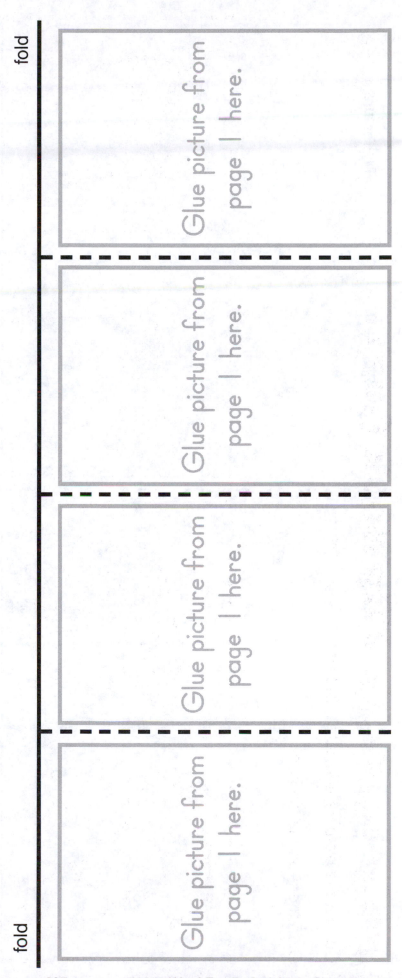

fold

Glue picture from page 1 here.

Glue picture from page 1 here.

Glue picture from page 1 here.

Glue picture from page 1 here.

fold

My Picture

My Picture

My Picture

My Picture

ug

ug

ug

ug

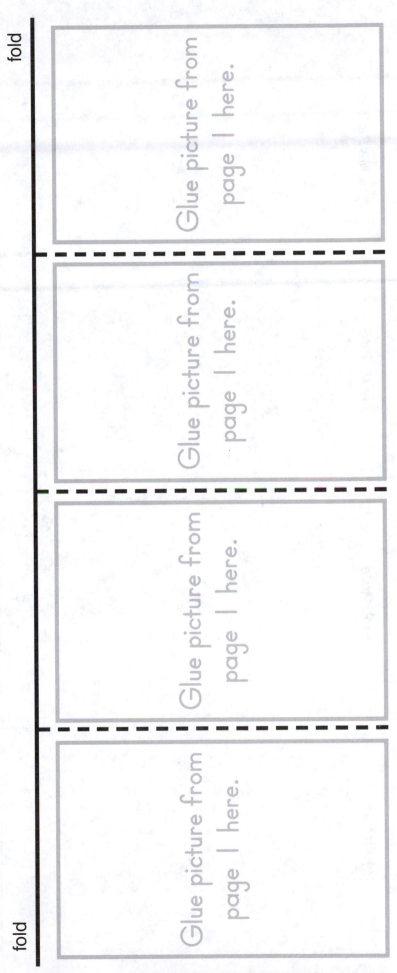

fold

Glue picture from page 1 here.

Glue picture from page 1 here.

Glue picture from page 1 here.

Glue picture from page 1 here.

fold

My Picture

My Picture

My Picture

My Picture

un

un

un

un

Flip Book (–un)

Cut out the pictures and letters below.

Glue them on the flip book.

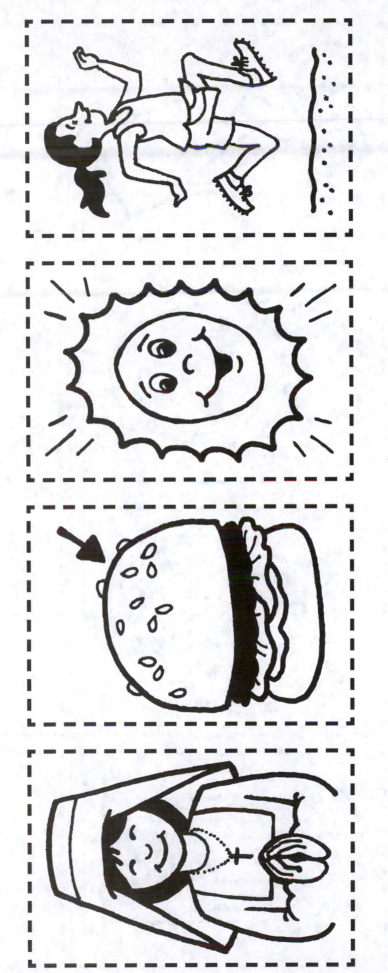

Flip Book (–ut)

Cut out the pictures and letters below.

Glue them on the flip book.

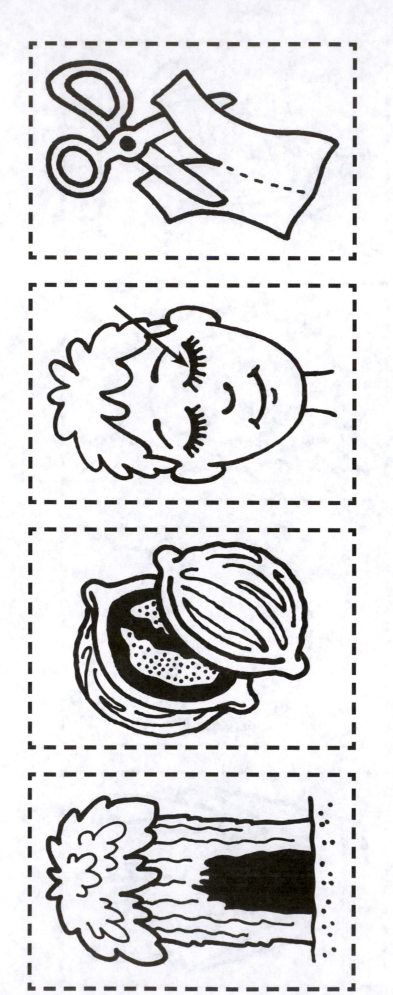

212

fold

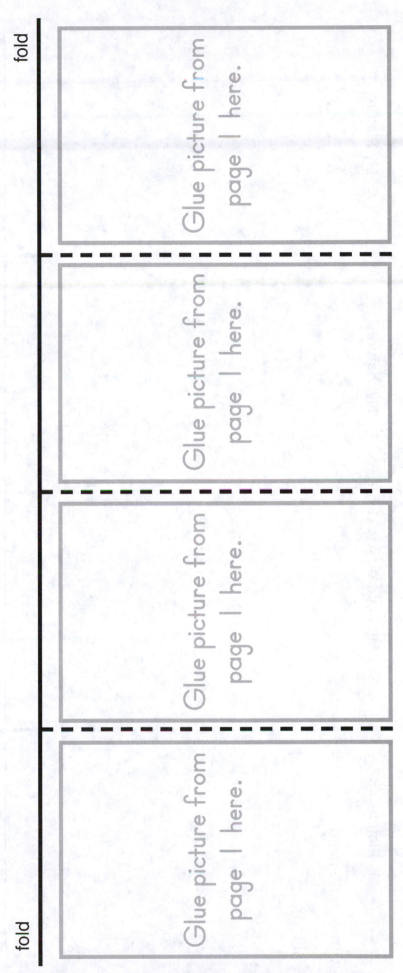

fold

My Picture

My Picture

My Picture

My Picture

ut

ut

ut

ut

Mystery Picture

Color the spaces with **–ug** pictures red to discover the mystery picture. Color the other spaces green.

Here is a _____ .

Mystery Picture

Color the spaces with **–un** pictures yellow to discover the mystery picture. Color the other spaces blue.

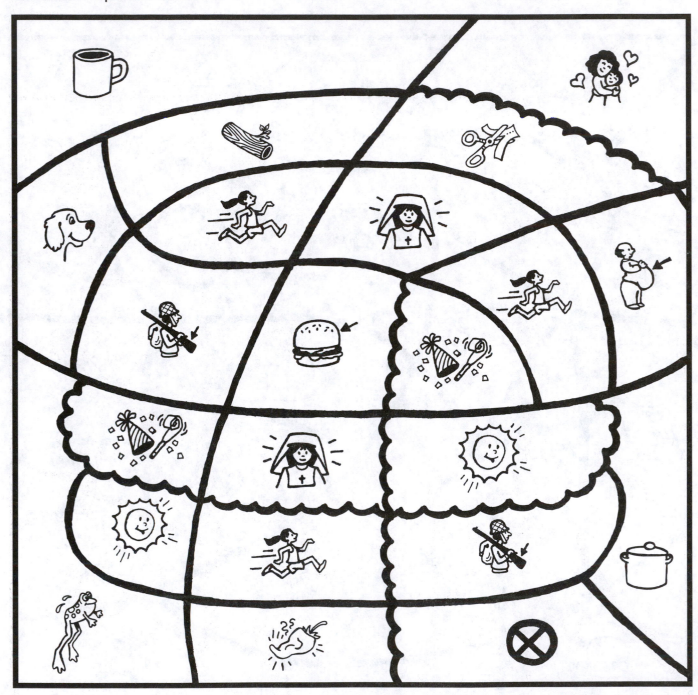

Here is a _____.

Mystery Picture

Color the spaces with **–ut** pictures yellow to discover the mystery picture. Color the other spaces blue.

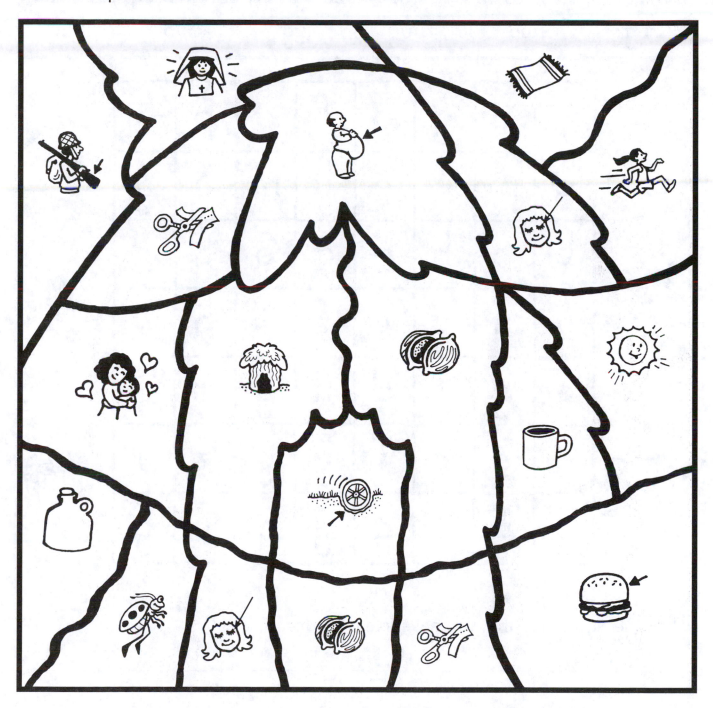

Here is a _____.

Word Search

Find and color the **–ug** words.

rug	hug	mug	jug	dug	bug

j	u	g	d	f	d	p	h
o	m	i	e	u	m	u	g
b	r	h	n	d	o	g	r
u	u	o	u	f	i	h	w
g	g	t	d	h	g	t	j
o	e	n	l	u	g	z	i
g	f	i	g	g	d	u	g

Write the **–ug** words that you have found above.

_____   _____   _____

_____   _____   _____

_____   _____   _____

_____   _____   _____

Word Search

Find and color the **–un** words.

bun	sun	fun	run	nun	gun

c	b	u	n	s	r	o	p
c	m	c	e	n	u	n	e
z	i	p	g	u	n	e	s
a	e	q	o	a	t	h	u
n	t	s	p	u	u	t	n
f	u	n	l	b	g	z	i
h	f	e	t	i	m	o	p

Write the **–un** words that you have found above.

_____   _____   _____

_____   _____   _____

_____   _____   _____

Word Search

Find and color the **–ut** words.

hut	cut	rut	gut	nut	shut

c	f	c	o	r	n	u	t
c	m	c	e	u	p	i	o
s	c	m	u	t	k	e	t
i	u	i	e	s	i	h	g
t	t	t	d	p	t	t	u
h	u	t	i	o	g	z	t
s	h	u	t	t	r	a	d

Write the **–ut** words that you have found above.

_____   _____   _____

_____   _____   _____

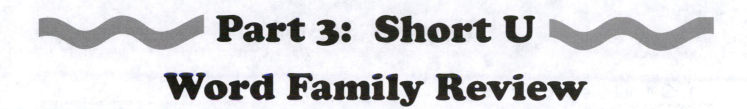

Part 3: Short U
Word Family Review

Activity Directions

Word Sort (pages 222 and 223)

Students will sort CVC words in the correct columns.

(*Extension:* Have students read the CVC words to classmates.)

Make, Read, and Write CVC Words (page 224)

Students cut out the letter and picture cards on the dashed lines. Students manipulate letter cards to form CVC words. Students then read the words and find the matching pictures. Lastly, students may use blank paper to write the CVC words they have found. Use plastic baggies or envelopes to store letters and pictures.

Fluency Practice (page 225)

Students read the randomly placed "short u" CVC words from top to bottom. Sand timers may be given to students to time how many words they can read in the given time.

My Own CVC Words (page 226)

Students will write their own "short u" CVC words on the lines provided. They can read and share their words with classmates.

(*Note:* Students can also cut on the solid lines to make flashcards.)

Making Sentences with CVC Words (pages 227, 228, or 229)

Students will cut out the "short u" CVC words and glue them in the boxes to make sentences. They can use the picture clues. Students should be encouraged to read their sentences aloud.

Word Sort

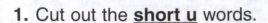

1. Cut out the **short u** words.

2. Glue each word in the correct column on the following page.

3. Be careful. There are some words that do not belong to the word families. Can you find them?

mud	bun	gut	shut	cut
hut	plum	run	dug	bus
plus	rut	jug	cup	sun
rug	fun	nut	pup	gum
up	mug	nun	bug	hug

-ug	-ut	-un

 # Make, Read, and Write CVC Words

Cut on the dashed lines. Make, read, and write **short u** words.

b	r	h	m	j
d	c	g	n	sh
s	f	sl	u	p
t	n			

Fluency Practice

Read → Read → Read → Read → Read →

hut	jug	bun	nut	mug	shut	fun	bug
run	mug	cut	shut	rut	hut	mug	hut
mug	nut	bug	rug	gut	cut	gut	sun
jug	dug	hug	rut	fun	sun	run	rug
nut	shut	cut	run	run	bun	jug	cut
gut	fun	fun	nut	nun	bug	nut	bun
sun	sun	hut	dug	jug	rug	nun	hug
rut	hug	run	fun	dug	hug	dug	rut

My Own CVC Words (short u)

CVC	CVC	CVC	CVC
CVC	CVC	CVC	CVC

Making Sentences with CVC Words

Cut out the **–ug** words below. Glue them in the correct boxes to create sentences. Read the sentences aloud.

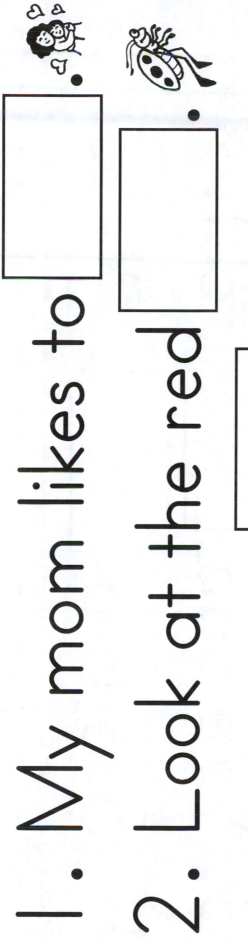

1. My mom likes to [ ].

2. Look at the red [ ].

3. I have a [ ].

4. Ben [ ] a pit.

---

mug

dug

bug

hug

Making Sentences with CVC Words

Cut out the –<u>un</u> words below. Glue them in the correct boxes to create sentences. Read the sentences aloud.

1. I like to have  .

2. I can play in the   .

3. We can  fast.

4. She is a  .

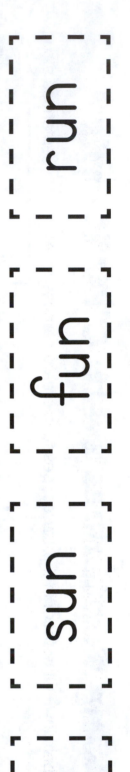

run

fun

sun

nun

Making Sentences with CVC Words

Cut out the –ut words below. Glue them in the correct boxes to create sentences. Read the sentences aloud.

1. [ ] your eyes.

2. Here is a 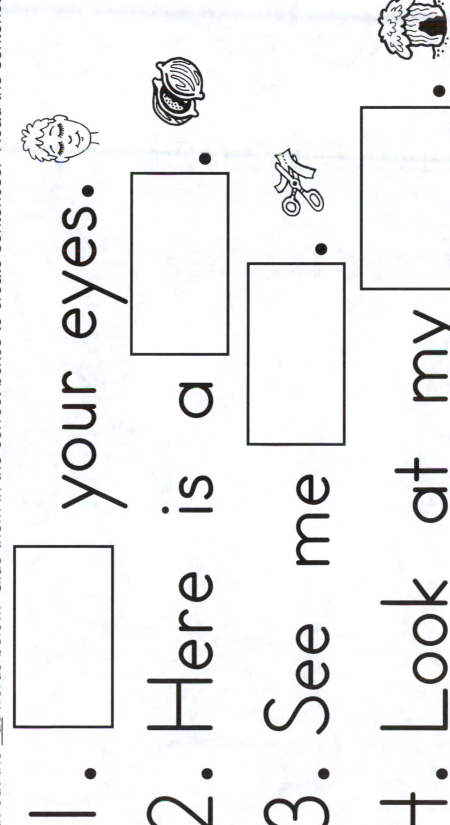 [ ].

3. See me [ ].

4. Look at my [ ].

cut   hut   Shut   nut

Additional Resources

Blending Boxes

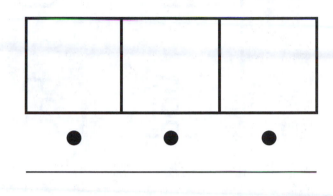

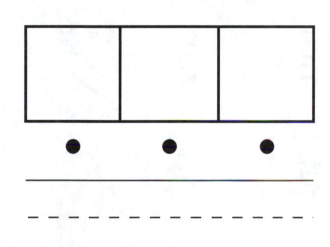
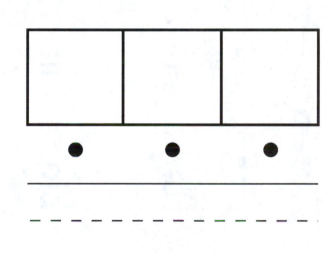

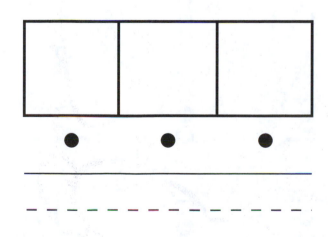
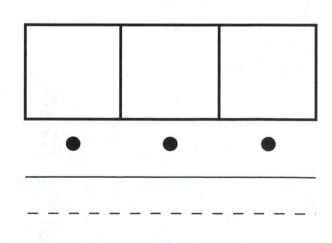

Mixed Fluency Practic

Read → Read → Read → Read →

mop	mug	fun	rut	sat	pan	lap
fed	men	net	big	lit	hog	pot
spot	jug	run	gut	mat	fan	nap	Ted
den	bet	fat	van	zap	shed	Ben	net
jig	hit	sip	jog	top	hot	dug	nun	nut

Mixed Fluency Practice

Read	Read	Read
dig	sit	bug	gun
shut	cat	frog	chop	cot	bun	cap
zip	cut	pig	rug	can	hit	pet	pot
hat	rig	hug	man	bed	dog	hen	stop	cut	red	map
bit	sun	dot	wet	hen	log	bat	fig

Mixed Fluency Practice

Read → Read → Read → Read →

mug	ran	kit	fun	lip	fed	fog	lap
hop	ten	not	jet	sat	big	jug	Ted
pan	mop	met	rut	men	lit	gut	spot
run	lap	chop	hot	dig	gun	nut	zap
sled	fat	frog	bet	van	bug	shut	top

Mixed Fluency Practice

Read → Read → Read → Read →

mat	jig	dug	fan	hit	nun	hog	shed
cot	den	nap	jog	Ben	tip	net	pop
rip	sit	cat	rut	dog	wet	sip	hen
chop	sun	hit	pig	zap	fed	Ben	dot
bug	zip	van	fat	sit	men	mop	shut

Mixed Fluency Practice

Read →   Read →   Read →   Read →

hat	tap	fog	pop	nun	jug	fig	kit
spot	shed	met	pan	fun	mat	dig	hog
net	cot	map	hop	cut	sled	frog	bit
tip	jet	can	sat	jog	not	rug	dip
nap	Ted	fan	hit	cut	top	pet	rig

Mixed Fluency Practice

← Read   ← Read   ← Read

cat	man	sled	ten	jet	pig	bit
dip	log	stop	pot	rug	bun	hut	hat
can	map	hen	bed	pet	rig	hit	zip
dog	pot	hug	dot	sun	cut	bat	ran
tap	red	wet	pen	fig	kit	lip	fog

Mixed Fluency Practice

Read → Read → Read → Read →

bit	fat	run	net	mug	top	van	gut	zap

tip | net | jug | spot | fed | pan | hog | Ted

dug | hot | cut | red | map | fig | dot | sun | zip

frog | chop | hit | stop | man | pig | bed | lit

jet | lap | hop | nun | shut | zap | fan | pop

Word Family Bingo

	FREE	

My Own CVC Words

CVC	CVC	CVC	CVC
CVC	CVC	CVC	CVC